PANDEMIC ORIGINS

PANDEMIC ORIGINS

QUINN SILVER

CONTENTS

Chapter 1: Introduction

The COVID-19 pandemic has irrevocably altered the course of global history. First identified in late 2019 in Wuhan, China, the novel coronavirus swiftly spread across the world, leading to widespread illness, death, and unprecedented social and economic disruption. As of now, millions have lost their lives, economies have suffered deep recessions, and entire societies have been transformed by the necessity of lockdowns, social distancing, and the ongoing quest for vaccination and treatment. The sheer scale and impact of this pandemic have led to a profound examination of its origins and the mechanisms that allowed it to propagate so widely and swiftly.

Understanding the origins of COVID-19 is not merely an academic exercise; it carries significant implications for public health, global cooperation, and the future of scientific research. The pandemic has underscored the vulnerabilities of our interconnected world and has sparked a pressing need to ascertain how such a virus could emerge. Was COVID-19 a naturally occurring virus that jumped from animals to humans, or is there a possibility that it was created or released deliberately? These questions are not just about scientific inquiry; they intersect with issues of political accountability, ethical responsibility, and international relations.

This book delves into the provocative theory that COVID-19 may have been created or released intentionally. While the prevailing narrative supports a natural origin, particularly a zoonotic spillover from wildlife to humans, there is an increasing body of evidence and speculation that warrants further exploration. The implications of such a theory could be staggering, raising concerns about biological weapons, biosecurity, and the integrity of global health systems.

In the chapters that follow, we will navigate through historical precedents of biological warfare, the early days of the pandemic, the role of the Wuhan Institute of Virology, and the competing theories surrounding the virus's origins. We will also examine the political, media, and public reactions that have shaped the discourse, the scientific investigations that have sought to uncover the truth, and the ethical considerations that arise from the handling of biological research.

As we embark on this exploration, it is crucial to approach the subject with a critical mind and an open heart, recognizing that understanding the origins of COVID-19 is vital for preventing future pandemics and ensuring a safer world for generations to come.

Chapter 2: Historical Context of Biological Weapon

The Evolution of Biological Warfare

Throughout history, humans have sought ways to exploit nature's deadliest forces in their pursuit of power, control, and survival. Among these methods, the use of biological weapons—living organisms or toxins derived from them to harm or kill adversaries—has a particularly dark legacy. The concept of using diseases as weapons is not new; it dates back centuries, arising from the simple observation that diseases could devastate armies, lay waste to cities, and even cripple entire nations. This section traces the evolution of biological warfare, examining how its roots emerged in ancient conflicts, how it transformed with scientific advancements, and how it remains a troubling facet of modern-day threats.

Early Instances of Biological Warfare

The earliest recorded use of biological agents in warfare comes from ancient times when diseased bodies or contaminated water sources were intentionally used to spread illness among enemies. For example, historical accounts suggest that as early as 400 BC, Scythian archers dipped their arrows in decomposed bodies and animal blood, introducing deadly infections to their opponents. Centuries later, in 1346, during the Siege of Caffa, Mongol forces reportedly hurled plague-infected corpses over the city walls to infect the defending soldiers and civilians. This incident is one of the earliest documented examples of biological warfare on a large scale, sparking fear and devastation as the Black Death spread across Europe shortly afterward.

Biological Warfare in the Middle Ages and Renaissance

As warfare evolved, so did the methods of delivering disease. During the Middle Ages, armies would sometimes resort to contaminating water supplies with animal carcasses or spreading disease-laden materials. The use of biological agents became a form of psychological warfare as much as a physical tactic, as fear of illness could often cause disorder and surrender. The Renaissance period saw the beginnings of more structured scientific thought, which eventually allowed for a deeper understanding of diseases and their transmission. However, the intentional use of disease remained a crude and horrific tactic, often used when direct confrontation was too costly or difficult.

The Shift Towards Scientific Weaponization

The 19th and early 20th centuries marked a shift in biological warfare. As medical science advanced, so did the potential for creating more sophisticated biological weapons. By the time World War I erupted, many nations had begun to explore the potential of using bacteria, viruses, and toxins as tools of war. Although chemical weapons overshadowed biological tactics during the war, the groundwork had been laid for future research into biological warfare. Scientists were beginning to understand how diseases spread, leading to the realization that pathogens could be harnessed as effective, if uncontrollable, weapons.

The Role of Microbiology in Weapon Development

The early 20th century also saw the rise of microbiology as a formal scientific discipline. The discovery of specific disease-causing microorganisms enabled military strategists to consider the use of these agents in a more controlled manner. For example, anthrax and botulinum toxin became subjects of study for their potential as lethal agents. With the outbreak of World War II, nations ramped up their biological warfare programs, developing more precise methods of deploying these agents and even conducting experiments on humans to assess their effects. The chilling legacy of Japan's Unit 731, which conducted inhumane experiments on prisoners, stands as a grim reminder of how scientific advancement can be turned toward devastating ends.

The Lingering Threat of Biological Warfare Today

Although international treaties have since sought to curb the use of biological weapons, their potential for destruction remains a present threat. Modern technological advancements have made it possible to manipulate biological agents in ways unthinkable just decades ago, raising concerns about the next generation of biological warfare. Understanding the historical evolution of these weapons is essential to comprehending the stakes today, as humanity faces an ongoing challenge: balancing scientific progress with the ethical responsibility to prevent its misuse. The history of biological warfare, a testament to both the ingenuity and destructiveness of human nature, provides critical lessons as we confront the potential risks of a new biological arms race.

Notable Historical Instances

The story of biological weapons is not simply a narrative of isolated events; it is an evolving history with recurring themes of secrecy, ambition, and the unintended consequences of scientific exploration. Biological agents have surfaced repeatedly in the annals of warfare, and their use has often been shrouded in mystery and controversy. In modern history, the two world wars and the subsequent Cold War era witnessed an acceleration in the development of biological weapons, as nations pushed scientific boundaries to gain an upper hand. This section examines some of the most notable instances in the history of biological warfare, from World War I to the Cold War, shedding light on how various powers sought to weaponize diseases to devastating effect.

World War I: Early Attempts at Weaponizing Disease

The First World War marked a period when both chemical and biological warfare began to be systematically explored. While chemical warfare stole the spotlight with deadly gases like chlorine and mustard gas, both sides quietly investigated the potential of biological agents. Germany, for instance, conducted covert operations to infect the horses and livestock used by Allied forces with anthrax and glanders, a bacterial disease capable of causing severe illness in animals and humans. The strategy was to disrupt the Allies' transportation and supply lines, making it harder for troops to access essential resources. Although biological warfare never reached the same prominence as chemical weapons during this period, these early experiments demonstrated the growing interest in harnessing biological agents for military purposes.

World War II and the Atrocities of Unit 731

By the time World War II erupted, the scientific understanding of pathogens had significantly advanced, leading to more deliberate efforts to develop biological weapons. In Japan, the notorious Unit 731, led by Lieutenant General Shiro Ishii, carried out some of the most heinous experiments on human subjects to test biological agents like plague, cholera, and anthrax. Japanese researchers subjected thousands of prisoners, primarily Chinese civilians, to lethal pathogens in field tests that sought to determine the viability of these diseases as weapons. They would release infected fleas or spread contaminated food and water in Chinese cities, leading to outbreaks that caused widespread suffering and death. Unit 731's experiments stand as a horrific example of wartime cruelty, one in which scientific research was warped into a tool of destruction.

Meanwhile, the Allied powers also pursued biological weapons research, although on a much smaller scale. The United States and the United Kingdom launched secret programs to explore the use of anthrax and botulinum toxin. In one particularly famous incident, the British government conducted experiments on the Scottish island of Gruinard, releasing anthrax spores to test their lethality on sheep. The island remained contaminated for decades afterward, underscoring the long-term dangers posed by biological agents. Although biological warfare was never employed on a large scale during World War II, the groundwork laid in these experiments would later fuel Cold War arms races.

The Cold War: An Era of Escalation and Stockpiling
The Cold War period saw an unprecedented escalation in biological weapons programs as the United States and the Soviet Union vied for global supremacy. Both superpowers developed massive stockpiles of biological agents, including anthrax, tularemia, and smallpox, with the capability to deploy them through missiles, aerial bombs, and other delivery mechanisms. The Soviet Union, in particular, maintained a vast biological weapons program under the codename "Biopreparat," producing and weaponizing pathogens at an alarming scale. Despite international treaties banning biological weapons, these clandestine programs continued, fueled by the mutual distrust and competitive ethos that defined the Cold War.

In the United States, the biological weapons program was run primarily out of Fort Detrick in Maryland. Researchers there developed various weaponized pathogens and delivery methods until President Richard Nixon officially terminated the program in 1969, leading to the eventual dismantling of the U.S. biological weapons arsenal. This move, largely in response to growing public concern over the ethics and potential consequences of biological warfare, marked a turning point. However, by this point, significant stockpiles had already been amassed, and the knowledge and materials could not be entirely erased.

The Impact of Biological Warfare on Civilian Populations

Throughout history, the use of biological agents in warfare has disproportionately affected civilian populations, spreading disease and fear among those far from the frontlines. The biological attacks conducted by Unit 731 in China and the anthrax tests on Gruinard Island had lasting effects on the health and well-being of entire communities. These instances illustrate how biological weapons blur the line between combatants and non-combatants, indiscriminately affecting everyone in their path. The threat of disease does not differentiate between military and civilian targets, and its psychological impact—generating fear, distrust, and social disorder—can be as devastating as its physical toll.

Biological Warfare's Legacy and Lessons

The historical instances of biological warfare serve as a reminder of the devastating potential of these weapons and the moral questions they raise. While the Cold War eventually led to the establishment of international treaties aimed at curbing the use of biological weapons, the legacy of their development continues to influence modern biosecurity policies. Understanding the use of biological weapons in World War I, World War II, and the Cold War provides critical insight into the lengths nations have gone to gain an advantage, even at the expense of ethics and humanity. As we confront the future of biological research, these lessons from history underscore the need for vigilance, transparency, and responsible scientific stewardship to prevent history from repeating itself in even more catastrophic forms.

International Treaties and Regulations

As the destructive potential of biological weapons became more evident, the international community recognized the urgent need for regulatory frameworks to prevent their proliferation. Biological agents are uniquely challenging because their effects can be devastating, unpredictable, and hard to contain, often impacting civilian populations far beyond the immediate battlefield. In response, global leaders have crafted treaties, conventions, and agreements designed to control and, ideally, eliminate biological warfare. These treaties, particularly the Biological Weapons Convention (BWC), reflect both the global commitment to preventing bioweapons use and the complexities of enforcing such regulations in an increasingly interconnected world.

The Genesis of Biological Weapons Control Efforts

The first steps toward international biological weapons control emerged in the early 20th century, alongside growing concerns about the weaponization of toxic substances and pathogens. In 1925, the Geneva Protocol was established, prohibiting the use of both chemical and biological weapons in warfare. Although a landmark achievement at the time, the Geneva Protocol had significant limitations: it banned the use of biological weapons but did not prevent countries from researching, developing, or stockpiling them. Moreover, the protocol lacked enforcement mechanisms, leaving nations free to interpret and sometimes ignore its provisions. As such, it served more as a symbolic statement against the horrors of biological warfare rather than a robust regulatory framework.

The Biological Weapons Convention (BWC)

In 1972, after decades of debate and increasing Cold War tensions, the international community established the Biological Weapons Convention (BWC), the first global treaty to ban an entire category of weapons. The BWC prohibits the development, production, and stockpiling of biological and toxin weapons and requires member states to destroy any existing stockpiles. The BWC marked a major step forward by not only prohibiting the use of biological weapons but also targeting their development at the source. As of today, more than 180 countries have ratified or acceded to the BWC, making it one of the most widely supported disarmament treaties.

Despite its groundbreaking framework, the BWC faces significant challenges. Unlike many other arms control treaties, the BWC lacks a formal verification mechanism, making it difficult to monitor and enforce compliance. This absence of oversight has led to concerns that some countries may continue to conduct prohibited research in secrecy. Efforts to introduce verification measures have been consistently blocked, primarily due to political disagreements and fears over sovereignty and security breaches. Thus, while the BWC represents a global consensus against biological weapons, it remains vulnerable to non-compliance.

Challenges in Regulating Biological Research and Dual-Use Technologies

One of the most pressing challenges in biological weapons control is regulating dual-use research—scientific work that has the potential for both beneficial and harmful applications. Advances in biotechnology, such as gene editing and synthetic biology, hold great promise for medicine and agriculture, but they also make it easier to create or modify pathogens for malicious purposes. This "dual-use dilemma" raises questions about how to promote scientific progress without inadvertently aiding bioweapons development. Some nations have adopted stringent controls and oversight on sensitive biological research, but these policies are not uniformly enforced across borders, creating gaps in global biosecurity.

To address these challenges, various initiatives have emerged to encourage responsible scientific conduct. The Australia Group, for example, is an informal alliance of countries that seeks to harmonize export controls on materials and equipment that could be used for biological weapons. Additionally, scientific organizations and institutions have begun to develop ethical guidelines and best practices to mitigate the risks of dual-use research. These efforts are steps in the right direction, but they rely heavily on voluntary compliance and the goodwill of individual researchers, leaving room for potential lapses.

Non-Proliferation Efforts and the Role of International Cooperation

Biological weapons are not confined by borders, and an outbreak caused by a bioweapon could rapidly become a global crisis. As such, international cooperation is essential to the BWC's success and to broader non-proliferation efforts. Agencies like the World Health Organization (WHO) and the United Nations have taken active roles in promoting awareness, fostering collaboration, and assisting countries in developing biosecurity protocols. The WHO, for instance, monitors global disease outbreaks and works to build healthcare capacities, aiming to detect and respond to suspicious events that might indicate a bioweapons attack. The United Nations, through its disarmament bodies, has encouraged transparency among member states and promoted confidence-building measures that aim to increase trust and accountability.

Despite these efforts, global cooperation remains fragile. Political tensions, economic rivalries, and national security concerns often impede collaborative progress, especially when it comes to sharing sensitive information about biological research. Recent discussions around updating the BWC have exposed divisions among member states, with some countries arguing for stricter controls and verification protocols, while others fear such measures could infringe on national sovereignty or hinder scientific advancement.

The Contemporary Challenges of Enforcement and Compliance

Even with international treaties in place, enforcement remains a major issue in biological weapons control. In contrast to chemical or nuclear weapons, biological agents can be developed with relatively modest resources and minimal infrastructure, making detection and regulation especially challenging. Unlike nuclear programs, which often require significant industrial facilities, bioweapons research can be conducted in small laboratories, often under the guise of legitimate medical or agricultural research. These factors make it difficult for international bodies to detect and respond to potential violations.

Some experts advocate for a revision of the BWC that would introduce verification measures, such as routine inspections or requirements for countries to report specific types of biological research. However, these proposals have faced opposition from several powerful nations, who argue that such measures would be intrusive and could expose sensitive information. This lack of enforceable verification continues to hamper the BWC's efficacy, highlighting the need for new approaches that balance transparency, security, and scientific freedom.

In summary, international treaties like the BWC represent a powerful global statement against the use of biological weapons, but they are not without flaws. The absence of verification mechanisms, coupled with the complexities of regulating dual-use research, creates ongoing challenges in achieving true biosecurity. As biological sciences advance and the risks associated with bioweapons grow, the international community faces a critical task: finding a way to strengthen these treaties, encourage compliance, and ultimately create a safer, more transparent global landscape.

Case Studies in Bioweapons Use and Accusations

Examining specific cases of bioweapons use and accusations throughout history offers critical insights into the complexity, controversy, and consequences of biological warfare. These cases reflect a range of motives—from strategic advantages in war to covert acts of sabotage—as well as the profound ethical and humanitarian concerns raised by bioweapons. They also reveal how accusations of bioweapons use can serve as powerful propaganda tools, sometimes clouding the truth and fueling suspicion between nations. This section explores some of the most significant and controversial instances of bioweapons use and accusations, from Cold War suspicions to more recent allegations, illustrating the far-reaching impact of biological warfare on international relations and public perception.

The Korean War: Allegations of Biological Warfare

One of the most contentious episodes in the history of bioweapons accusations occurred during the Korean War. In the early 1950s, North Korea and China accused the United States of deploying biological weapons against North Korean and Chinese forces, alleging that American aircraft dropped disease-carrying insects and contaminated materials to spread deadly pathogens, including plague and cholera. These allegations were accompanied by graphic descriptions and purported evidence of the pathogens' effects, sparking outrage and fear throughout Asia. The U.S. government vehemently denied these accusations, labeling them as communist propaganda designed to discredit American military operations.

Despite numerous investigations, the truth behind these accusations remains inconclusive. Some historians and researchers argue that the allegations were part of a Cold War-era psychological warfare campaign by the Soviet Union, intended to undermine the United States' global image. Others suggest that there may have been some basis for the claims, citing classified U.S. military documents that discuss the potential use of biological agents. Regardless of their veracity, the Korean War allegations exemplify how accusations of bioweapons use can be weaponized in their own right, serving as tools to damage reputations and stir international controversy.

The "Yellow Rain" Controversy in Southeast Asia

During the 1980s, reports emerged of a mysterious "yellow rain" that allegedly caused severe illnesses and death among villagers in Southeast Asia, particularly in Laos and Cambodia. The United States accused the Soviet Union of supplying toxins to its allies in the region, specifically implicating a compound known as T-2 mycotoxin, a toxic substance produced by certain fungi. According to reports from refugees and local witnesses, aircraft would release a yellow, sticky substance that appeared to be causing symptoms like bleeding, respiratory distress, and death.

The U.S. government quickly pointed to the Soviet Union as the source of these bioweapons, igniting a wave of global outrage. However, subsequent investigations cast doubt on these claims. In the late 1980s, scientists began to question whether the "yellow rain" was, in fact, a natural phenomenon—specifically, bee droppings laced with pollen, which could appear yellow and sticky under certain conditions. This revelation complicated the narrative, highlighting the challenges of verifying bioweapons use and the ease with which misinterpretations can occur. Although the exact nature of "yellow rain" remains uncertain, this case underscores the potential for error and confusion in bioweapons accusations, as well as the broader political implications of such allegations.

The Sverdlovsk Anthrax Incident

One of the most well-documented cases of biological weapons use occurred not in a battlefield, but in a Soviet city. In 1979, an outbreak of anthrax swept through the city of Sverdlovsk (now Yekaterinburg), killing at least 66 people and infecting many others. Initially, Soviet authorities attributed the outbreak to contaminated meat, denying any connection to biological warfare. However, defectors and Western intelligence agencies raised suspicions that the outbreak was linked to a secret Soviet bioweapons program. It was later revealed that the Sverdlovsk incident resulted from an accidental release of anthrax spores from a military research facility, where anthrax was being produced as part of the Soviet Union's extensive bioweapons program.

The Sverdlovsk incident exposed the dangers of biological research conducted in secrecy and underscored the potential for catastrophic consequences from accidental releases of deadly pathogens. It also strained Soviet-U.S. relations, as the incident fueled Western fears about the scope and ambition of the Soviet Union's bioweapons capabilities. Decades later, the Sverdlovsk case continues to serve as a stark reminder of the risks associated with biological weapons research and the long-term health and diplomatic impacts of even a single lapse in biosecurity.

The Gulf War and Iraq's Alleged Biological Arsenal

In the early 1990s, as tensions mounted between Iraq and the Western world, concerns emerged over Iraq's alleged possession of biological weapons. Under the regime of Saddam Hussein, Iraq was believed to have developed an arsenal of bioweapons, including anthrax and botulinum toxin, as part of a broader weapons of mass destruction (WMD) program. The 1991 Gulf War and subsequent inspections by the United Nations Special Commission (UNSCOM) uncovered evidence suggesting that Iraq had, in fact, pursued biological weapons capabilities. However, the extent of this arsenal remained unclear, as many facilities were destroyed or dismantled during and after the war.

The Gulf War served as a catalyst for increased global scrutiny of bioweapons programs, especially in volatile regions. It underscored the need for international inspection and verification mechanisms to prevent the proliferation of biological weapons. The Iraq case also highlighted the limitations of relying on intelligence alone to assess a country's bioweapons capabilities, as conflicting information and the challenges of verifying compliance led to ongoing disputes within the international community. Ultimately, Iraq's alleged bioweapons program became a focal point in the discourse around WMDs, setting the stage for future conflicts and raising questions about the effectiveness of international regulations.

Recent Allegations: The Syrian Civil War and ISIS

In recent years, allegations of biological weapons use have resurfaced, particularly in the context of the Syrian Civil War and the rise of extremist groups like ISIS. Reports suggest that ISIS militants may have attempted to develop and deploy rudimentary biological agents, such as ricin, to instill fear and disrupt local populations. Although these attempts appear to have been largely unsuccessful, they reveal the potential for non-state actors to pursue biological weapons, even with limited resources and technical expertise.

The Syrian Civil War has also raised concerns about the possible use of bioweapons by the Assad regime. While most reports focus on chemical weapons, there have been unverified claims of biological agents being considered or tested. This situation underscores the dual threat posed by biological weapons: not only are state actors capable of developing and deploying them, but non-state groups with ideological motivations or terrorist ambitions may also seek to harness pathogens as weapons. The involvement of extremist groups highlights the urgent need for global vigilance and cooperation to prevent bioweapons from falling into the hands of those who might use them with little regard for humanitarian consequences.

In reflecting on these case studies, it becomes clear that accusations of biological weapons use carry weighty political, humanitarian, and ethical implications. From Cold War rivalries to modern conflicts involving non-state actors, each case demonstrates the inherent risks of biological warfare and the challenges associated with verification and accountability. Understanding these historical examples provides a foundation for assessing contemporary biosecurity threats and reinforces the importance of maintaining stringent international safeguards against bioweapons proliferation.

The Ethical and Humanitarian Concerns Surrounding Biological Warfare

Biological weapons not only threaten national security and public health but also pose profound ethical and humanitarian questions. The use of these weapons crosses a moral threshold, raising complex issues about the nature of warfare, the value of human life, and the responsibilities of scientific communities. Unlike conventional weapons, biological agents can spread uncontrollably, potentially affecting generations, devastating ecosystems, and violating fundamental principles of humanity and ethics in warfare. This section delves into the ethical challenges posed by bioweapons, examining their disproportionate impact on civilian populations, the enduring health effects, and the moral dilemmas associated with research that could potentially facilitate biological warfare.

The Disproportionate Impact on Civilians

The most alarming aspect of biological warfare is its inevitable impact on civilians, who are often caught in the crossfire of bioweapons deployment. Unlike traditional weapons, which can be aimed at specific military targets, biological agents are much harder to control and contain, often resulting in unintended casualties among non-combatants. An airborne pathogen or a waterborne virus, for instance, does not distinguish between soldier and civilian, child or adult. As diseases spread, they can decimate populations, disrupt local economies, and overwhelm healthcare systems ill-equipped to handle outbreaks of this magnitude.

From an ethical standpoint, this indiscriminate harm to civilian populations represents a grave violation of the principle of distinction, a core tenet of international humanitarian law, which mandates that combatants distinguish between military targets and non-combatants. Biological weapons make such distinctions nearly impossible to uphold, challenging the very notion of a "just" war and deepening the moral implications of their use. Moreover, the long incubation periods of many pathogens mean that those exposed to bioweapons may unknowingly carry infections to new areas, creating a ripple effect that can persist well beyond the initial deployment zone, compounding the suffering of innocent people.

The Long-Term Health and Environmental Consequences

Bioweapons leave lasting scars, not only on the immediate victims but also on future generations and the environment. Pathogens and toxins can cause chronic illnesses, genetic mutations, and psychological trauma that persist long after the weapons themselves have been deployed. For instance, survivors of anthrax attacks have reported lifelong respiratory problems and an increased risk of certain cancers, underscoring the enduring human toll of bioweapons. Similarly, viral agents can alter entire ecosystems by killing off keystone species or infecting animal populations, thereby destabilizing food sources and biodiversity.

The environmental impact of biological warfare further complicates the ethical landscape. In some cases, diseases introduced by bioweapons could eliminate animal populations, destroy plant life, or contaminate water sources, leading to ecological imbalances that are difficult, if not impossible, to reverse. This type of ecological damage has far-reaching effects, from diminishing agricultural productivity to driving species to extinction. For communities that depend on these ecosystems for survival, the consequences are devastating, leading to food shortages, displacement, and long-term poverty. The intergenerational nature of this harm raises questions about humanity's obligation to preserve the planet for future generations and the ethical responsibilities scientists and governments hold in preventing irreversible ecological harm.

The Ethical Dilemma of Dual-Use Research

One of the most significant ethical challenges associated with biological weapons is the dual-use dilemma—the fact that research conducted to advance medical and scientific knowledge can also be used to develop deadly weapons. Fields such as virology, genetics, and synthetic biology hold immense potential for improving human health but also offer pathways for creating highly contagious or lethal pathogens. This overlap forces scientists, institutions, and governments to confront difficult questions: How can we encourage beneficial scientific research while preventing its misuse? What safeguards are needed to ensure that discoveries intended to save lives do not end up costing them?

Various scientific bodies have proposed ethical guidelines for dual-use research, encouraging transparency, oversight, and responsible conduct among researchers. Some have suggested that scientists should adopt a code of conduct that prohibits work on bioweapons and requires adherence to strict biosecurity protocols. However, these measures rely heavily on voluntary compliance and cannot guarantee that research won't be misappropriated. In a world where knowledge travels easily across borders, it is challenging to restrict or monitor dual-use research effectively, especially when commercial and academic institutions operate within diverse regulatory environments. This ethical quandary forces society to continually balance the advancement of science with the potential for unintended, catastrophic consequences.

Moral Responsibility and the Role of International Governance

The potential for biological weapons to cause harm on a massive scale underscores the need for a unified international stance on bioethics and bioweapons regulation. Many experts argue that countries have a moral responsibility to participate in global efforts to prevent the development and deployment of bioweapons, as the consequences of such actions extend beyond national borders. Organizations like the United Nations and the World Health Organization have attempted to create frameworks that promote transparency, ethical research, and accountability in the realm of biological sciences, urging nations to comply with the Biological Weapons Convention (BWC) and adopt stringent biosecurity measures.

However, international governance is inherently limited by political divisions and differing national interests, making it challenging to enforce bioethics standards consistently across countries. In some cases, geopolitical tensions have led nations to question the motives of others, hindering collaboration and creating an atmosphere of mistrust. This underscores the moral responsibility of not only governments but also individual scientists and institutions to prioritize ethical standards in their work. Ultimately, a truly effective framework requires cooperation, trust, and a shared commitment to preventing harm, emphasizing the need for both top-down regulation and grassroots adherence to bioethical principles.

Public Health Ethics and the Preparedness Paradox

Another ethical consideration in biological warfare is the "preparedness paradox"—the dilemma faced by public health officials in preparing for potential bioweapons attacks without encouraging the very research that could lead to their creation. Investing in biodefense measures and creating stockpiles of vaccines and antidotes is essential for national security, but it also implies the possibility of bioweapons deployment. This paradox raises questions about where to draw the line between necessary preparedness and unintended facilitation of bioweapons development.

Public health ethics also emphasize the duty of governments to protect their citizens from biological threats, which complicates the issue further. While preparing for bioweapons attacks is prudent, there is an ethical risk of fostering an arms race, where nations justify offensive biological research in the name of defense. Additionally, prioritizing biodefense could potentially detract from efforts to address more immediate public health concerns, such as infectious diseases that already exist. This balancing act forces policymakers to weigh the benefits of preparedness against the moral risks, recognizing that an overemphasis on biodefense might inadvertently normalize or encourage the notion of bioweapons as a legitimate tool of warfare.

The Legacy of Biological Warfare and the Imperative for Ethical Vigilance

The use of biological weapons not only leaves physical and psychological scars but also challenges society to confront its own ethical boundaries. As science advances and new biotechnologies emerge, the potential for biological warfare expands, demanding an equally rigorous ethical response. The legacy of biological warfare—from ancient toxins to modern gene-editing techniques—illustrates the profound and lasting consequences of using life itself as a weapon. It serves as a reminder of the thin line between scientific progress and moral compromise, emphasizing the importance of ongoing ethical vigilance.

Understanding these ethical and humanitarian concerns is essential for preventing future misuse of biological knowledge. It underscores the imperative for a global consensus on bioethics, reinforced by strong regulatory frameworks, dedicated international oversight, and a commitment to responsible science. The ultimate goal is to ensure that advancements in biology and medicine continue to benefit humanity, without enabling the horrors of biological warfare. Only by prioritizing ethical considerations at every level—from individual scientists to international bodies—can society hope to navigate the complex moral landscape of biological weapons and prevent history's mistakes from being repeated.

Chapter 3: Early Days of the Pandemic

The Emergence of COVID-19 and First Cases

In late 2019, as the world prepared to enter a new decade, the residents of Wuhan, a sprawling city in Hubei Province, China, were about to experience an unprecedented upheaval. The earliest reports of a mysterious illness surfaced in December, centered around individuals who had frequented the Huanan Seafood Wholesale Market. Symptoms ranged from fever and fatigue to severe respiratory distress, leading local hospitals to report an unusual spike in pneumonia cases. As healthcare workers scrambled to treat those affected, they noticed a disturbing pattern—this was not a typical seasonal illness, nor did it respond to conventional treatments.

On December 31, 2019, Chinese authorities reported a cluster of pneumonia cases to the World Health Organization (WHO), identifying the likely origin of the outbreak at the seafood market. The exact cause remained unknown, and initially, the virus was believed to be zoonotic, meaning it likely transferred from animals to humans. However, it would take weeks before scientists identified this novel pathogen as a coronavirus, one that would later be named SARS-CoV-2. This virus, unlike those that caused the common cold or even the first SARS outbreak in 2003, showed signs of being highly infectious, transmitting easily between people.

As January began, Chinese authorities took initial steps to contain the spread, including shutting down the seafood market. The public, however, remained largely unaware of the virus's potential for widespread transmission. Doctors and nurses in Wuhan bore the first wave of infections, with some reportedly becoming ill themselves—a strong indication that human-to-human transmission was occurring. Yet, without concrete evidence, public health officials hesitated to confirm this risk publicly, and life continued mostly as normal in Wuhan, albeit with growing concern among healthcare workers.

In mid-January, the virus continued to spread silently, and cases began to appear outside of Wuhan, in other parts of China and eventually internationally, including Thailand and Japan. As it became evident that the virus was not confined to Wuhan, local health officials and scientists rushed to understand its characteristics, but significant questions remained. How contagious was this virus? What was its fatality rate? And most critically, how had it emerged so suddenly?

By January 20, 2020, a Chinese epidemiologist publicly confirmed that human-to-human transmission was indeed occurring. This admission marked a critical shift in understanding the virus's potential to spread globally. Shortly after, Wuhan went into an unprecedented lockdown, effectively sealing off a city of over 11 million people. The lockdown, which would extend to surrounding areas, was a dramatic step, one that signaled the severity of the threat posed by this unknown virus.

In the days that followed, public health experts worldwide closely monitored the situation, with some expressing doubts about the virus's origins. Although much focus remained on the Huanan

Seafood Market as a possible source, suspicions also arose about whether the virus could have accidentally emerged from a laboratory setting, given Wuhan's proximity to the Wuhan Institute of Virology, which conducted research on coronaviruses. This alternative theory, while lacking evidence at the time, sparked interest and became a topic of discussion among both scientists and the public.

The early days of COVID-19 were marked by a combination of uncertainty and urgency. While the virus spread quickly and invisibly across borders, local and global responses took shape gradually, as public health officials, scientists, and governments scrambled to comprehend the nature of this new threat. These early developments set the stage for what would become a historic pandemic, one that would test the resilience, resources, and resolve of communities worldwide.

Initial Reactions and Public Health Warnings

As January unfolded, the world began to turn its attention to the virus brewing in Wuhan. News of a mysterious pneumonia-like illness spread through international health agencies and media, sparking initial curiosity and concern. On January 9, 2020, the World Health Organization (WHO) released its first statement about the "pneumonia cases of unknown cause" reported in Wuhan, noting that Chinese scientists had isolated a new type of coronavirus. This announcement, though cautious, highlighted the need for vigilance as health authorities around the globe began to take stock of the emerging threat.

Within China, local and national health officials were moving quickly to contain the virus. In addition to the closure of the Huanan Seafood Market, officials introduced measures aimed at identifying and isolating new cases, encouraging people to seek medical help if they experienced symptoms. However, this period was marked by mixed messaging, with the general public and some government figures not yet recognizing the full gravity of the situation. Public health advisories focused on routine hygiene practices, while the underlying threat of human-to-human transmission remained uncertain, adding to the challenge of establishing effective public health responses early on.

Despite these efforts, by mid-January, cases had surfaced beyond Wuhan, with new infections reported in Beijing, Shenzhen, and other major Chinese cities. It was evident that COVID-19 was no longer confined to a single location. Neighboring countries quickly took notice, with South Korea, Japan, and Thailand reporting their first cases among travelers returning from Wuhan. International airports began implementing screening measures, targeting passengers arriving from China to identify potential cases and contain further spread. This marked one of the earliest global public health interventions against COVID-19, as governments introduced travel advisories and started implementing basic containment strategies.

On January 22, 2020, the WHO convened an emergency committee to determine whether the outbreak constituted a "public health emergency of international concern" (PHEIC). Though the organization refrained from making an official declaration at that point, urging countries to continue monitoring the situation closely, the meeting highlighted the urgency of coordinated international action. As the virus continued to spread, countries like the United States began to issue travel restrictions and advisories, reflecting a growing realization that COVID-19 could reach epidemic proportions. By this time, confirmed cases had already spread to Europe, North America, and beyond, underscoring the virus's ability to cross borders with ease.

The public response in various countries mirrored a spectrum of reactions, from indifference and skepticism to mounting anxiety. In Asia, where nations had experienced previous outbreaks such as SARS and MERS, governments and citizens responded with heightened caution. In contrast, regions with limited recent exposure to such outbreaks took longer to appreciate the potential severity. For instance, while Taiwan, Hong Kong, and South Korea rapidly implemented widespread testing and quarantine measures, other countries initially treated the virus as a localized problem in China, underestimating its global implications.

By the end of January, the WHO officially declared COVID-19 a public health emergency of international concern. This designation, which had only been applied a few times before, signaled that the outbreak posed a significant risk not only to affected areas but to global health and safety. Countries worldwide were urged to coordinate and step up their public health responses, ranging from border control and quarantine protocols to ramping up testing and contact tracing. As the world entered February, the urgency to contain COVID-19 had become unmistakable, with governments, health agencies, and the public adjusting to the unsettling reality of a virus that could reach anyone, anywhere.

This period of initial responses and public health warnings highlighted both the strengths and vulnerabilities in the global health system. As each country faced mounting pressure to protect its citizens, early actions—or lack thereof—played a critical role in shaping the trajectory of the pandemic. The speed and scope of international cooperation, combined with public health strategies that varied widely from one region to the next, would soon reveal a landscape where coordination, transparency, and swift action were essential. This initial stage set the foundation for the complex interplay of science, politics, and public health that would dominate the world's response to COVID-19 in the months to come.

Initial Reactions and Public Health Warnings

As January unfolded, the world began to turn its attention to the virus brewing in Wuhan. News of a mysterious pneumonia-like illness spread through international health agencies and media, sparking initial curiosity and concern. On January 9, 2020, the World Health Organization (WHO) released its first statement about the "pneumonia cases of unknown cause" reported in Wuhan, noting that Chinese scientists had isolated a new type of coronavirus. This announcement, though cautious, highlighted the need for vigilance as health authorities around the globe began to take stock of the emerging threat.

Within China, local and national health officials were moving quickly to contain the virus. In addition to the closure of the Huanan Seafood Market, officials introduced measures aimed at identifying and isolating new cases, encouraging people to seek medical help if they experienced symptoms. However, this period was marked by mixed messaging, with the general public and some government figures not yet recognizing the full gravity of the situation. Public health advisories focused on routine hygiene practices, while the underlying threat of human-to-human transmission remained uncertain, adding to the challenge of establishing effective public health responses early on.

Despite these efforts, by mid-January, cases had surfaced beyond Wuhan, with new infections reported in Beijing, Shenzhen, and other major Chinese cities. It was evident that COVID-19 was no longer confined to a single location. Neighboring countries quickly took notice, with South Korea, Japan, and Thailand reporting their first cases among travelers returning from Wuhan. International airports began implementing screening measures, targeting passengers arriving from China to identify potential cases and contain further spread. This marked one of the earliest global public health interventions against COVID-19, as governments introduced travel advisories and started implementing basic containment strategies.

On January 22, 2020, the WHO convened an emergency committee to determine whether the outbreak constituted a "public health emergency of international concern" (PHEIC). Though the organization refrained from making an official declaration at that point, urging countries to continue monitoring the situation closely, the meeting highlighted the urgency of coordinated international action. As the virus continued to spread, countries like the United States began to issue travel restrictions and advisories, reflecting a growing realization that COVID-19 could reach epidemic proportions. By this time, confirmed cases had already spread to Europe, North America, and beyond, underscoring the virus's ability to cross borders with ease.

The public response in various countries mirrored a spectrum of reactions, from indifference and skepticism to mounting anxiety. In Asia, where nations had experienced previous outbreaks such as SARS and MERS, governments and citizens responded with heightened caution. In contrast, regions with limited recent exposure to such outbreaks took longer to appreciate the potential severity. For instance, while Taiwan, Hong Kong, and South Korea rapidly implemented widespread testing and quarantine measures, other countries initially treated the virus as a localized problem in China, underestimating its global implications.

By the end of January, the WHO officially declared COVID-19 a public health emergency of international concern. This designation, which had only been applied a few times before, signaled that the outbreak posed a significant risk not only to affected areas but to global health and safety. Countries worldwide were urged to coordinate and step up their public health responses, ranging from border control and quarantine protocols to ramping up testing and contact tracing. As the world entered February, the urgency to contain COVID-19 had become unmistakable, with governments, health agencies, and the public adjusting to the unsettling reality of a virus that could reach anyone, anywhere.

This period of initial responses and public health warnings highlighted both the strengths and vulnerabilities in the global health system. As each country faced mounting pressure to protect its citizens, early actions—or lack thereof—played a critical role in shaping the trajectory of the pandemic. The speed and scope of international cooperation, combined with public health strategies that varied widely from one region to the next, would soon reveal a landscape where coordination, transparency, and swift action were essential. This initial stage set the foundation for the complex interplay of science, politics, and public health that would dominate the world's response to COVID-19 in the months to come.

Escalation to a Global Crisis

In the early months of 2020, what had initially been perceived as a regional health issue swiftly transformed into a global crisis of unprecedented scale. COVID-19 had broken free of geographical boundaries, infiltrating every continent and spreading through major cities across the world. By the end of February, it was clear that the virus was no longer a distant concern limited to isolated outbreaks but a direct threat to communities worldwide. Countries scrambled to respond to the escalating emergency, even as they struggled to comprehend the virus's full impact and transmission patterns. What started as an epidemic had grown into a pandemic, revealing weaknesses in public health systems and global preparedness.

Italy was among the first Western countries to experience a severe outbreak. The virus took root in Lombardy, a densely populated region with bustling economic activity, where it spread quickly and overwhelmed local healthcare facilities. Hospitals in cities like Bergamo and Milan were soon flooded with patients struggling to breathe, and medical personnel faced shortages of ventilators, protective gear, and even basic supplies. Italy became a harbinger of what lay ahead, with haunting images of patients lined up in hospital corridors and military convoys transporting coffins out of cities that could no longer cope. As Italy implemented one of the strictest lockdowns in modern history, other European nations began preparing for what many feared was inevitable.

Across the Atlantic, the United States watched the crisis unfold with a growing sense of urgency. Despite initial optimism that it might be able to contain any potential outbreak, the virus began spreading in communities across the country, most notably in New York City, which would become the pandemic's epicenter in the U.S. By March, hospitals there were on the brink, struggling to manage a surge of patients and reporting widespread shortages of personal protective equipment. With healthcare systems strained, Americans faced a sobering realization that the virus had silently infiltrated daily life, and extensive measures were needed to prevent further devastation. States began to enact lockdowns, schools transitioned to online learning, and workplaces were forced to adapt to remote operations almost overnight.

Around the world, the virus exploited the interconnectedness of modern society. From Europe to Asia, Africa to the Americas, countries faced critical challenges as they worked to limit the spread.

Global air travel, a key driver of the virus's rapid transmission, was heavily restricted. Airports, train stations, and major hubs of transportation ground to a halt as nations enforced border closures and imposed strict travel bans. This unprecedented shutdown of global movement marked the beginning of a prolonged disruption to international business, tourism, and trade, with supply chains and economies strained under the weight of restrictions.

In response to the burgeoning crisis, the World Health Organization officially declared COVID-19 a pandemic on March 11, 2020. This pronouncement underscored the virus's uncontrolled spread and alerted governments worldwide to take decisive action. Countries launched national emergency responses, many mobilizing military personnel to aid in testing and health service logistics, while others began implementing widespread public health campaigns encouraging social distancing, mask-wearing, and rigorous hygiene practices. Media outlets bombarded the public with information, advice, and updates as the collective fight against COVID-19 intensified.

However, the strain on healthcare systems was not uniform. Wealthier nations with robust medical infrastructure were able to mobilize resources relatively quickly, while lower-income countries faced significant obstacles in accessing essential supplies, testing, and treatment. The pandemic highlighted a stark divide in global health equity, as wealthier nations raced to stockpile protective gear, ventilators, and eventually vaccines, while others struggled with a shortage of even the most basic healthcare resources. Organizations like the WHO and other non-profits stepped in to offer assistance, but the enormity of the crisis revealed glaring gaps in global preparedness and collaboration.

As COVID-19 cases continued to escalate worldwide, the full scope of the pandemic began to reveal itself—not just as a medical crisis, but as a transformative event reshaping the social, economic, and political landscape. Countries faced unparalleled challenges in balancing the health of their populations with the pressing need to mitigate economic fallout. Many nations entered a cycle of restrictive lockdowns followed by brief reopenings, only to reimpose lockdowns as new waves of infections surged. This rhythm of uncertainty underscored the resilience and adaptability required of individuals, communities, and institutions as they navigated an uncharted path through the pandemic.

In the span of a few short months, COVID-19 had irrevocably altered the world, disrupting life as we knew it and testing the foundations of modern society. The initial phase of the crisis exposed vulnerabilities that many had not anticipated and highlighted the urgent need for a united, coordinated approach to confront a truly global threat. The escalating spread of the virus forced a reckoning with long-held assumptions about public health, resilience, and global solidarity, setting the stage for what would become a prolonged and profound struggle against an invisible adversary.

Initial Theories on COVID-19's Origin

As COVID-19 swept across the globe, the urgent need to understand its origin became a focal point of scientific inquiry and public interest. The rapid, unprecedented spread of the virus raised questions about how a pathogen of this scale and impact could have emerged so suddenly. At the heart of the debate were two main theories: the natural origin theory, which suggested that COVID-19 had transferred from animals to humans in a wildlife market, and the lab-leak theory, which posited that the virus might have accidentally escaped from a laboratory engaged in coronavirus research. Both theories sparked intense debate within scientific circles and among the general public, each carrying significant implications for global health and policy.

The first theory, the natural origin hypothesis, traced back to the early reports linking the outbreak to the Huanan Seafood Wholesale Market in Wuhan. In many cases, coronaviruses have zoonotic origins, meaning they transfer from animals to humans, often through an intermediary species. SARS-CoV, which caused the SARS outbreak in 2003, is believed to have passed from bats to civet cats before infecting humans, and MERS-CoV, another coronavirus, emerged from camels. Given this pattern, scientists initially hypothesized that SARS-CoV-2, the virus causing COVID-19, had similarly jumped from bats or another wildlife species to humans, likely in a high-contact setting like the seafood market.

This theory was supported by initial genetic analyses of SARS-CoV-2, which showed a close resemblance to other coronaviruses found in bats. However, despite intensive research, scientists were unable to identify a specific intermediary species that would bridge the transmission from bats to humans. Without concrete evidence tracing the virus to a specific animal host, the natural origin theory left gaps that fueled alternative explanations. While the zoonotic theory remained the mainstream scientific perspective, the lack of a definitive link between SARS-CoV-2 and an intermediary species left room for public speculation and scientific debate.

Parallel to the natural origin theory was the lab-leak hypothesis, which drew attention due to the Wuhan Institute of Virology's (WIV) proximity to the outbreak's epicenter. The WIV is one of the world's leading research institutions on bat coronaviruses, with scientists there having conducted extensive studies on SARS-like viruses in bats. The coincidence of a novel coronavirus outbreak occurring in a city with a lab known for such research prompted questions about whether an accidental leak could have occurred.

While there was no immediate evidence to support this theory, it gained traction as some scientists, journalists, and government officials pointed out the possibility of a research-related mishap.

The lab-leak theory was further fueled by reports of past safety concerns at similar high-level research facilities, known as BSL-4 labs, where the most dangerous pathogens are studied. While the vast majority of such facilities maintain strict safety protocols, even a minor lapse could theoretically result in an accidental release. Proponents of the lab-leak hypothesis pointed to reports of potential lapses in safety standards at the WIV, although these claims were not substantiated. Advocates of this theory argued that even a small probability of a lab-based origin warranted thorough investigation, given the pandemic's monumental impact.

Throughout the early days of the pandemic, both theories were weighed by scientists, policymakers, and the media. As the pandemic grew, the lab-leak theory, once regarded as a fringe idea, started to receive more serious consideration, partly because of the scientific community's inability to pinpoint an intermediary species. The debate over COVID-19's origins became not only a scientific issue but also a matter of geopolitical tension, particularly as countries around the world experienced the devastating toll of the virus. Questions about transparency, accountability, and the responsibilities of research institutions took center stage, making the issue of COVID-19's origins a matter of both public interest and political significance.

The search for COVID-19's origins revealed more than just the story of the virus itself; it highlighted the challenges of scientific research in a world of heightened political sensitivities. While scientific inquiry has always aimed for objective truth, the charged atmosphere surrounding COVID-19 made neutrality difficult, with competing interests and biases often influencing public narratives. The debate underscored the importance of transparency in scientific research and the need for open, international collaboration, especially when investigating matters of global health.

Ultimately, as COVID-19 continued to spread, the quest to understand its origins became a race against time, not only to solve a scientific puzzle but also to prevent future outbreaks. With both theories representing distinct but plausible explanations, the question of COVID-19's origins remained one of the most critical—and contentious—issues of the pandemic. Scientists around the world committed to rigorous research and evidence-based conclusions, hoping that with time, careful investigation, and open communication, they might bring the world closer to understanding how this devastating virus first made its way into human society.

The World Responds to the Unknown

As the threat of COVID-19 became undeniable, nations worldwide mobilized with unprecedented urgency. Governments, health organizations, and scientists raced to respond to a virus that was both mysterious and deadly. The initial wave of lockdowns, quarantines, and travel restrictions marked a unified effort to "flatten the curve" and prevent hospitals from becoming overwhelmed. But despite these measures, the virus continued its relentless spread, exposing the limitations and disparities in global preparedness for pandemics.

Countries implemented varied strategies in response to the crisis. Some, like South Korea and New Zealand, quickly adopted aggressive testing, contact tracing, and isolation protocols, which helped them contain outbreaks in their early stages. Others, like the United States and several European nations, struggled with inconsistent policies and delayed responses that allowed the virus to gain a stronger foothold. The rapid and unpredictable spread of COVID-19 put intense pressure on public health systems, with shortages of personal protective equipment (PPE), ventilators, and ICU beds becoming common across the globe.

In many parts of the world, healthcare workers found themselves on the front lines of a battle they were ill-equipped to fight. Hospitals in hard-hit areas were soon operating at or beyond capacity, forcing medical staff to make difficult decisions about allocating limited resources. These harrowing conditions took a profound toll on frontline workers, who faced not only physical exhaustion but also the emotional burden of caring for patients in isolation, as families were often prohibited from visiting. Images of overworked doctors and nurses became a poignant symbol of the pandemic's human cost, underscoring the need for robust support systems and mental health resources for healthcare professionals.

The economic ramifications of the pandemic were equally profound. As countries enforced lockdowns and social distancing measures, businesses shuttered, supply chains were disrupted, and unemployment soared. The economic downturn triggered by COVID-19 reached a scale not seen since the Great Depression, affecting industries from tourism to manufacturing to retail. Millions of individuals and families around the world faced financial hardship, with many countries forced to implement emergency stimulus measures to provide relief to citizens and businesses. Yet, these measures were often stopgaps, unable to fully compensate for the pandemic's lasting economic impact.

At the same time, scientists and pharmaceutical companies around the world launched an unprecedented effort to develop a vaccine. The speed and scale of this endeavor were unparalleled, with research teams collaborating across borders, sharing data, and conducting accelerated clinical trials. While vaccine development typically spans several years, COVID-19 catalyzed a global response that saw the first vaccines authorized for emergency use within a year of the virus's discovery. This monumental scientific achievement offered a glimmer of hope, demonstrating the potential of international cooperation and the resilience of human ingenuity in the face of crisis.

The pandemic also prompted a reevaluation of the role of international organizations in managing global health threats. The World Health Organization (WHO), tasked with coordinating responses and providing guidance, became a focal point for both support and criticism. While the WHO played a key role in sharing information, advising on containment strategies, and coordinating vaccine distribution through initiatives like COVAX, it faced scrutiny over its initial response to the outbreak and its relationship with member states. Questions emerged regarding the WHO's autonomy, funding, and ability to navigate the complex political dynamics that influence global health decisions.

Public trust in governmental and scientific authorities was another casualty of the pandemic. As lockdowns, mask mandates, and later vaccine rollouts were implemented, misinformation and skepticism spread widely, fueled by social media and conflicting reports. Conspiracy theories regarding the virus's origins and the motives of public health measures gained traction, complicating efforts to achieve broad compliance with health guidelines. The battle against COVID-19 became as much an issue of public perception as it was a medical challenge, revealing the importance of clear, transparent communication from leaders and scientists alike.

COVID-19 did more than disrupt daily life; it exposed vulnerabilities and fault lines in societal structures, from healthcare to economics to international relations. In the face of unprecedented uncertainty, the global response revealed both the strengths and weaknesses of our interconnected world. Communities showed resilience, supporting each other through acts of kindness and solidarity, while nations reevaluated their health infrastructure, supply chains, and crisis preparedness. The lessons of COVID-19 underscored the need for stronger global health systems, a renewed commitment to public health, and a unified approach to preventing future pandemics.

The early days of the pandemic set the tone for what would become an enduring global challenge. The virus, once unknown and underestimated, reshaped every facet of life, forcing societies to adapt, innovate, and rebuild. As the world continues to grapple with COVID-19's aftermath, the lessons learned from this pandemic will shape the future of public health, policy, and international cooperation, leaving an indelible mark on humanity's approach to managing crises in the years to come.

Chapter 4: The Wuhan Institute of Virology

Background on the Wuhan Institute of Virology (WIV)

The Wuhan Institute of Virology (WIV) stands as one of the world's most notable research facilities focused on infectious diseases, with a particular emphasis on virology and viral genetics. Founded in the 1950s, the WIV has evolved over the decades from a modest research facility into a leading institute within the Chinese Academy of Sciences, earning its status as China's premier virology lab. Located in the city of Wuhan, a metropolis with a dense population and bustling trade, the WIV has become an essential part of China's infectious disease research, geared toward identifying, tracking, and analyzing pathogens with pandemic potential.

Since its inception, the WIV's mission has been rooted in addressing and understanding viral threats, particularly those emerging from China's rich biodiversity. Given the country's vast variety of wildlife and proximity to regions where human-animal contact is common, the potential for zoonotic diseases—illnesses that transfer from animals to humans—has always been a significant public health concern. Understanding this risk, the WIV established itself as a pioneering institute in cataloging viral genomes, studying virus-host interactions, and developing tools to respond to emerging infectious diseases. Its research portfolio includes studies on severe viral pathogens, including the Nipah virus, Ebola, and various strains of influenza, but it is particularly known for its work on coronaviruses, including those found in bats.

One of the most critical milestones in WIV's journey was the establishment of a Biosafety Level-4 (BSL-4) lab in 2015, the first of its kind in mainland China. BSL-4 labs are designed to study the most dangerous pathogens known to humankind, those with a high fatality rate for which there are often limited treatments or vaccines. These labs are equipped with strict safety protocols and containment measures, such as air-locked doors, specialized protective gear, and rigorous decontamination processes, allowing researchers to study pathogens safely without risking exposure to the surrounding community. The BSL-4 facility at WIV quickly became a cornerstone of China's infectious disease preparedness strategy and elevated the institute's global standing, enabling it to engage in cutting-edge research and to join a small, elite group of institutions worldwide with the capability to handle high-level biological threats.

As a top-tier research facility, the WIV fostered collaborations with a range of international scientists, universities, and health organizations. Through partnerships with institutions in the United States, Europe, and Australia, the WIV engaged in research projects designed to prepare for and prevent future pandemics. These collaborations often involved data sharing, joint studies, and participation in international conferences focused on infectious diseases. The WIV's research on SARS-like coronaviruses in bats was particularly valued by global health officials, as it contributed to the international understanding of viral reservoirs and transmission dynamics that could lead to human outbreaks.

For years, the WIV held a reputation as a beacon of scientific achievement and a model of China's advancements in virology and disease prevention. Its scientists, many of whom had trained at top international universities, were recognized as leaders in their fields. Among them was Dr. Shi Zhengli, an expert in bat-borne viruses who would come to be known as "China's Bat Woman" for her pioneering work in tracing coronaviruses in bats. The institute's growing expertise in this area not only bolstered its reputation but also positioned it at the center of discussions on zoonotic transmission, a field of increasing importance as globalization and environmental changes heighten the risk of pandemics.

Yet, the prominence of WIV in virology research would eventually draw intense scrutiny with the onset of the COVID-19 pandemic, given the institute's proximity to the first reported cases. While WIV's background and objectives were once lauded internationally, they would become points of controversy, as the lab's focus on coronaviruses raised questions about the virus's origins and potential connections to its research activities. The institute's longstanding position in the heart of China's scientific community and its work on coronaviruses would thus thrust it into a global spotlight as the search for COVID-19's origins began, underscoring the complex interplay between scientific research, public health, and international relations.

Research Conducted at WIV Prior to the Pandemic

In the years leading up to the COVID-19 pandemic, the Wuhan Institute of Virology (WIV) had been on the cutting edge of virus research, with an emphasis on coronaviruses found in bats. This focus was no coincidence. China's diverse ecosystems and proximity to wildlife habitats created an environment ripe for zoonotic viruses—diseases that can be transmitted from animals to humans. Recognizing the public health risk posed by zoonotic viruses, the WIV prioritized studies that could uncover how these pathogens emerged, spread, and adapted to new hosts, including humans.

One of the most significant figures in WIV's research on coronaviruses was Dr. Shi Zhengli, a renowned virologist whose expertise in bat-borne viruses earned her international acclaim. Dr. Shi and her team focused on identifying and categorizing viruses in bat populations, with particular attention to coronaviruses similar to SARS-CoV, the virus responsible for the 2002-2003 SARS outbreak. Her team's fieldwork took them to remote caves where bat colonies thrive, and their painstaking efforts led to the discovery of hundreds of coronavirus strains. This research became the basis of numerous studies published in leading scientific journals, advancing global understanding of coronaviruses and their zoonotic potential.

The institute's work on coronaviruses wasn't merely academic; it was driven by the urgent need to prevent another SARS-like outbreak. By studying how coronaviruses evolve and adapt, researchers hoped to identify which strains might pose the greatest risk of crossing over to humans. Dr. Shi's team analyzed genetic sequences and tracked how these viruses used specific proteins to infect cells, with a focus on the spike protein, which allows coronaviruses to bind to receptors in host cells. This research was instrumental in understanding how certain coronaviruses might adapt to human hosts and provided insight into how viral mutations could increase infectivity or alter transmission dynamics.

A key area of WIV's coronavirus research involved what is known as "gain-of-function" studies. This controversial line of research involves genetically altering viruses to study potential mutations that might make them more infectious or deadly. Proponents argue that gain-of-function research helps scientists anticipate and mitigate the risks posed by naturally occurring pathogens. By manipulating viruses in a controlled environment, researchers aim to understand which mutations would make a virus more likely to jump from animals to humans or spread rapidly within human populations. However, this type of research also carries risks; even with rigorous safety protocols, accidents can occur, leading to concerns that such research, if not managed carefully, could result in unintended exposure to dangerous pathogens.

Before COVID-19, the WIV's research on SARS-like coronaviruses, including gain-of-function experiments, was widely accepted as critical work within the virology community. Its studies were supported by major health organizations and funders, including the National Institutes of Health (NIH) in the United States, as part of international efforts to prepare for potential pandemics. The institute's database of viral genomes, which documented thousands of bat coronavirus strains, was considered an invaluable resource for global health, as it provided crucial information that could help detect and respond to new viral threats.

The importance of this research extended beyond China. WIV's findings on coronaviruses were shared with scientists worldwide, contributing to a better understanding of the biological mechanisms that underlie pandemics. Scientific publications from the institute were frequently cited, and WIV researchers presented their findings at international conferences, fostering an atmosphere of collaboration and knowledge-sharing. Prior to the pandemic, the WIV's research program was seen as a proactive effort to prevent future outbreaks and support global health security. It was also viewed as an example of how Chinese scientists were making substantial contributions to the international scientific community.

Despite the groundbreaking nature of WIV's work, its focus on coronaviruses would become a focal point of controversy with the emergence of COVID-19. The institute's vast database of bat coronaviruses and its history of gain-of-function experiments drew attention as scientists and governments sought to understand the origins of the virus. What had once been a celebrated area of research was now under intense scrutiny, as questions arose about whether WIV's experiments, even with the intention of preventing pandemics, might have inadvertently contributed to the very event it sought to avert.

The WIV's research legacy, which once represented China's commitment to scientific excellence, would be reevaluated in light of COVID-19. The debate over gain-of-function research, which had simmered for years among scientists and policymakers, would intensify as the pandemic unfolded, bringing the institute's work on bat coronaviruses into an international debate. This shift reflected a profound change in how the world viewed not only the WIV but also the balance between scientific ambition and the ethical boundaries of research in an age where the stakes were higher than ever before.

International Collaboration and Funding

The Wuhan Institute of Virology (WIV) was not merely a national lab conducting isolated research in China; it was part of a larger network of global scientific collaboration. In the years leading up to the COVID-19 pandemic, WIV formed partnerships with several international research institutions and health organizations, making it a central player in the global virology community. Funding and expertise from institutions in the United States, Australia, and Europe supported WIV's work on emerging infectious diseases, which many scientists and governments recognized as an international priority given the increasing threat of global pandemics. These collaborations involved shared data, joint publications, and in some cases, co-funding of critical research projects that advanced under-standing of zoonotic viruses, especially coronaviruses.

One of WIV's most prominent international partnerships was with the U.S.-based EcoHealth Alliance, a non-governmental organization focused on the study and prevention of emerging infectious diseases. EcoHealth Alliance, led by Dr. Peter Daszak, had an established reputation for its research on zoonotic viruses in animal populations, especially in bat species known to harbor coronaviruses. Through this partnership, EcoHealth Alliance and WIV received joint funding from the National Institutes of Health (NIH) in the United States to study bat coronaviruses and assess their potential to cause future pandemics. This collaboration aimed to catalog viral strains, understand virus transmission dynamics, and identify which viruses had the genetic potential to adapt to human hosts. The partnership allowed WIV to work with cutting-edge technology and methodology, much of it provided through NIH-funded projects, and to share findings that would inform pandemic preparedness strategies worldwide.

The scope of WIV's collaboration extended beyond EcoHealth Alliance. Researchers from the WIV regularly worked with scientists from top laboratories in Australia and Europe, many of whom contributed their own resources, expertise, and funding to advance WIV's work. For instance, the lab received funding and technical support from the Pasteur Institute in France to enhance its virology research capabilities. French scientists were also instrumental in the initial construction of WIV's BSL-4 laboratory, providing training in biosafety procedures and helping the lab adhere to international standards for high-containment research. Such collaborations were not just scientific but were seen as strategic investments in global health, intended to enhance response capabilities to emerging infectious diseases.

With these partnerships, the WIV also became a key contributor to data-sharing initiatives focused on viral genomes. In the years leading up to the pandemic, WIV researchers published numerous studies in international journals and provided genomic data on bat coronaviruses to public databases. This open sharing was intended to aid other scientists in recognizing potential zoonotic threats, fostering a transparent research environment. Through these publications and data-sharing efforts, WIV played a significant role in enhancing the global understanding of how coronaviruses evolved and spread, insights that were essential in modeling potential outbreaks and improving preventive measures. Many scientists and public health officials applauded WIV for its willingness to share such valuable data, which formed part of the foundation for predictive research on pandemics.

These partnerships and funding arrangements positioned WIV as a key player in international pandemic preparedness, and its work on bat coronaviruses became widely respected within the virology community. However, the international collaborations and funding also meant that WIV's research practices were held to high standards by both the scientific community and funding entities. The NIH and other funders required WIV to adhere to strict research protocols and ethical standards, including routine audits and transparency about research goals and methods. These funding bodies often placed stipulations on research grants, ensuring that laboratories like WIV followed rigorous guidelines designed to minimize risks, particularly when dealing with potential pandemic pathogens.

Nevertheless, these close ties with foreign institutions would later become a point of contention when questions surrounding COVID-19's origins arose. The international funding and support, once seen as symbols of trust and cooperative progress, were reexamined through a lens of suspicion. The collaboration with EcoHealth

Alliance, in particular, became a focus of controversy in the United States, with critics questioning whether American tax dollars indirectly funded gain-of-function research—experiments that could potentially increase a virus's infectivity or transmissibility. Although the NIH maintained that its funds were not intended for high-risk gain-of-function studies, the debate over WIV's research practices and its ties to global institutions intensified, bringing scrutiny to the once-celebrated partnerships.

In retrospect, the collaboration between WIV and international research entities underscores the complexities of global science in a world where infectious diseases do not recognize borders. While the partnerships were initiated with the intent of advancing science and preparing for future pandemics, they later ignited debates over research ethics, safety, and transparency. These collaborations, which had once been emblematic of progress in pandemic preparedness, ultimately became part of the larger discourse on the origins of COVID-19, adding a layer of international tension to what had once been a story of shared scientific endeavor.

Allegations and Theories about the Lab's Involvement in the Virus's Release

As COVID-19 spread across the globe, questions about the virus's origins began to intensify. While initial reports suggested a possible link to the Huanan Seafood Wholesale Market in Wuhan, where live animals were sold, some researchers and political figures turned their attention to the Wuhan Institute of Virology (WIV). The proximity of the institute to the first known cases of COVID-19, combined with its research on bat coronaviruses, led to speculation that the virus could have escaped from WIV, whether by accident or through an intentional act. These suspicions gave rise to a highly controversial theory: that COVID-19 was not merely a zoonotic spillover but potentially the result of a lab incident or even a deliberate act.

One of the earliest proponents of the lab-origin theory was a group of scientists and officials who believed the unique characteristics of SARS-CoV-2—the virus responsible for COVID-19—warranted an investigation into whether it could have been manipulated in a laboratory setting. They pointed to the virus's high transmissibility and its particular affinity for human ACE2 receptors, which some argued appeared to be unusually well-suited for human infection. The idea of a lab leak wasn't initially grounded in conclusive evidence; instead, it was a hypothesis driven by the perceived gaps in the natural origin theory and the coincidental location of the WIV near the outbreak's epicenter.

Adding to the suspicion were reports that WIV researchers had been conducting gain-of-function experiments on coronaviruses. These experiments, intended to enhance scientific understanding of how viruses evolve to infect humans, involved modifying viruses to make them more infectious or transmissible under controlled conditions. While the goal of such studies was to predict potential zoonotic spillovers and improve pandemic preparedness, they were inherently risky, as any accidental exposure or containment failure could theoretically lead to an outbreak. WIV scientists, including Dr. Shi Zhengli, maintained that all research was conducted with appropriate safety protocols in place, but questions about biosafety practices in China, particularly in BSL-3 and BSL-4 laboratories, fueled speculation.

International attention to these theories was heightened by statements from officials in both the United States and Europe. For instance, in early 2020, U.S. Secretary of State Mike Pompeo and President Donald Trump publicly hinted that they had seen intelligence pointing to a possible lab origin for the virus, though no specific evidence was shared. The Trump administration's stance intensified interest in the lab-origin theory, as did revelations that some researchers at WIV had reportedly fallen ill with COVID-19-like symptoms shortly before the first identified cases in Wuhan. This detail, though never fully verified, further fanned the flames of speculation, casting doubt on the assurances of lab safety provided by Chinese authorities and scientists.

The Chinese government responded to these accusations by firmly denying any possibility of a lab leak and asserting that the virus had a natural origin. Chinese officials highlighted a report by the World Health Organization (WHO) that concluded it was "extremely unlikely" the virus had escaped from a lab, though this assessment was later criticized by some international experts as being heavily influenced by Chinese authorities. China's stance was that WIV had adhered to strict international safety standards and that their research had contributed to global virology efforts rather than endangering them. Nonetheless, China's lack of transparency regarding early COVID-19 data, restricted access to original patient records, and a refusal to allow independent inspections of WIV added further credibility to the theory for skeptics.

In addition to government officials, several prominent scientists and public figures weighed in on the possibility of a lab leak. The publication of a letter in *The Lancet* in early 2020 by a group of scientists, who denounced the lab-leak theory as a conspiracy and reaffirmed their support for WIV's integrity, initially appeared to quash the debate. However, it later emerged that the letter had been organized by EcoHealth Alliance President Dr. Peter Daszak, whose organization had funded WIV research, sparking accusations of conflict of interest. The revelation cast doubt on the objectivity of certain scientific responses, leading some to believe that there had been a concerted effort to suppress open discussion about the lab-leak hypothesis.

Over time, the lab-origin theory morphed from fringe speculation into a subject of legitimate scientific inquiry. Researchers and officials called for further investigation into the origins of SARS-CoV-2, including access to WIV records and databases that had been taken offline early in the pandemic. Although the WHO conducted a limited investigation into the origins of COVID-19 in 2021, critics argued that the scope was insufficient and that key data were withheld. Some experts urged for a more independent investigation, free from political influence, to conclusively determine whether the virus had a natural origin or had emerged from a laboratory setting.

As the debate around the lab-origin theory continued, it became apparent that this question transcended science, carrying profound political and ethical implications. For China, the suggestion of a lab leak represented an existential threat to its credibility on the world stage and raised concerns about accountability and transparency. For the international community, especially Western nations, confirming or disproving the lab-leak theory was critical not only for understanding COVID-19 but also for preventing similar outbreaks in the future. This lingering uncertainty over WIV's possible involvement became emblematic of the larger geopolitical rifts that the pandemic had exposed, leaving the world divided not only on the origins of COVID-19 but on the principles of scientific openness and responsibility.

In summary, while no conclusive evidence has emerged to prove the lab-origin theory, the ongoing scrutiny of WIV reflects the global desire for answers about COVID-19's origins. What began as a theory based on proximity and perceived gaps in data evolved into a topic of global debate, raising fundamental questions about the balance between scientific progress and ethical boundaries. Whether or not WIV was involved in the virus's release, the allegations underscored the need for transparency, rigorous safety standards, and global cooperation in scientific research, particularly when it comes to studying pathogens with pandemic potential.

The Impact of Speculation on Science and Global Relations

The speculation surrounding the Wuhan Institute of Virology (WIV) and the origins of COVID-19 has had far-reaching effects on the scientific community and international relations. What began as questions about the origins of a novel virus quickly grew into a global debate that has since shifted perceptions of scientific transparency, the responsibilities of research institutions, and the balance of trust between nations. Regardless of whether COVID-19 originated from a laboratory or from nature, the scrutiny and allegations have influenced science policy, international diplomacy, and the broader societal trust in research—particularly in fields related to infectious disease.

One of the most immediate effects of the lab-origin speculation has been a significant shift in how governments and the public perceive high-stakes scientific research, particularly in virology. The debate over the lab-leak theory has led to a reevaluation of certain practices, especially those related to gain-of-function research, where scientists modify pathogens to understand their transmission potential and prepare for possible outbreaks. For decades, this type of research was largely accepted within the scientific community as necessary to stay ahead of evolving threats. However, with the emergence of SARS-CoV-2, questions have arisen over whether the risks of such research outweigh the potential benefits. The heightened scrutiny of WIV and similar labs worldwide has prompted calls for increased oversight and transparency, with scientists and policymakers advocating for stricter regulations around pathogen research. In response, some nations have reviewed and even suspended specific research projects, illustrating a shift toward more caution in scientific endeavors involving dangerous pathogens.

The controversy has also complicated international collaboration on infectious disease research. Prior to the pandemic, global partnerships were viewed as essential to combating health threats that transcend borders, allowing scientists to pool resources, expertise, and data. However, the intense focus on WIV and its international connections has strained some of these relationships, particularly between the United States and China. Accusations over data withholding, limited access to original samples, and perceived lack of transparency from Chinese authorities have fostered distrust, complicating efforts to collaborate effectively. Additionally, the blame game between nations over the origins of COVID-19 has underscored the geopolitical dimensions of science. It's become evident that research is not only a means of advancing human knowledge but also a tool of influence, with countries vying for both control over information and international credibility.

Beyond government actions, the public response to the origins debate has also highlighted evolving attitudes toward scientific institutions. In a world where information spreads rapidly, sometimes without vetting or context, speculation about WIV has fueled various narratives—some grounded in legitimate inquiry, others in conspiracy theories. This spread of information has created an environment where public trust in science is fragile. On the one hand, the pandemic underscored the importance of scientific research in tackling health crises, as seen in the rapid development of vaccines. On the other hand, the unanswered questions about COVID-19's origins have made some people question the integrity of research institutions and whether scientific discoveries are always shared transparently. This duality has highlighted the need for a more open scientific process, one that the public feels they can trust.

The effects of the origins debate extend further into international health policy and funding. Many countries are now reconsidering how and where they fund research, particularly in fields that involve cross-border collaboration. Governments and funding agencies are increasingly demanding more transparency from research institutions and, in some cases, implementing new requirements for data sharing and safety measures as conditions for funding. For example, the United States has introduced stricter guidelines for federally funded research involving pathogens, especially in labs operating abroad. These changes signify a renewed focus on accountability and an acknowledgment that, as science becomes increasingly global, so too must its standards. These policy adjustments reflect a commitment to public safety but also indicate a shift toward greater self-reliance, with some countries opting to develop domestic research capabilities to reduce dependence on foreign institutions.

Finally, the ongoing speculation and investigation into COVID-19's origins have underscored the ethical complexities involved in biological research. Scientists around the world are confronting difficult questions about the moral implications of their work, particularly in fields that carry inherent risks. In response to the pandemic, bioethics discussions have taken center stage, prompting researchers to carefully consider not only the potential benefits of their studies but also the potential consequences. The discussions around WIV have served as a reminder that scientific innovation must be accompanied by ethical responsibility, particularly when dealing with infectious diseases that have the capacity to spread globally. This emerging focus on ethics in science is likely to have long-lasting impacts, shaping future research protocols and en-

couraging scientists to approach their work with a heightened awareness of its possible societal impact.

In conclusion, the WIV controversy has left a lasting impact
on both science and geopolitics. The questions raised about
COVID-19's origins have driven significant changes in research policies, international relations, and public perceptions of science. The
desire for greater transparency and accountability has spurred policy
shifts, led to new safety protocols, and fueled an ongoing dialogue
about the ethical responsibilities of researchers. While the definitive
origins of COVID-19 remain unknown, the incident has provided
a critical lesson: scientific research, especially in areas as sensitive as
virology, requires not only rigorous methods but also a global commitment to openness and trust. This balancing act—between innovation and safety, between cooperation and independence—will
likely continue to shape the future of science in a post-COVID
world, influencing how we respond to emerging health threats and
how we view the interconnected nature of global research.

Chapter 5: The Natural Origin Theory

Overview of the Natural Origin Theory

The natural origin theory is one of the primary explanations for how SARS-CoV-2, the virus responsible for COVID-19, came into existence and spread among humans. This theory suggests that SARS-CoV-2 was transmitted from animals to humans through a process known as zoonosis. Zoonotic transmission refers to the movement of pathogens from animals to humans, a phenomenon well-documented in epidemiology. Many viruses affecting humans today, including Ebola, HIV, and earlier coronaviruses like SARS-CoV and MERS-CoV, emerged through zoonotic events, making the natural origin theory a plausible explanation for COVID-19.

The core idea of this theory is that SARS-CoV-2 likely originated in bats, which are known to harbor a vast diversity of coronaviruses. This theory is further strengthened by the fact that other coronaviruses, like SARS-CoV, also share an origin in bats. The virus would then have passed through one or more intermediate animal hosts before finally jumping to humans. An intermediate host acts as a bridge, allowing viruses to adapt to new environments and potentially increase in infectivity when interacting with human physiology. The identification of such an intermediate species has been a central question in the search for COVID-19's origins.

The zoonotic process is a complex one, influenced by various environmental and ecological factors. Human activities, such as deforestation, urban encroachment into wildlife habitats, and the trade of wildlife, increase the likelihood of zoonotic spillovers by bringing humans into closer contact with animal reservoirs of viruses. Markets where live animals are sold, known as "wet markets," are believed to be particularly conducive to zoonotic transmission, as they house multiple species in close proximity. This environment allows pathogens to move across species more easily, creating a possible path for viruses like SARS-CoV-2 to reach humans.

Several researchers have pointed to previous coronavirus outbreaks as supporting evidence for the natural origin theory. The SARS outbreak in 2003 and the MERS outbreak in 2012 both demonstrated that coronaviruses can successfully make the leap from animals to humans, especially in environments where animals and humans closely interact. In the case of SARS, the virus was traced back to bats and civet cats, while MERS was found to have passed through camels as an intermediary. These outbreaks offer a blueprint for how coronaviruses can emerge and spread in human populations, providing a logical framework for considering a similar pathway for SARS-CoV-2.

This view is also grounded in substantial genetic evidence. Studies of SARS-CoV-2's genome reveal similarities with other coronaviruses found in animal populations, specifically bats and pangolins. By analyzing the virus's genetic structure, scientists have found that it shares approximately 96% of its genetic code with a known bat coronavirus. This finding has reinforced the idea that SARS-CoV-2 has a natural origin rather than a human-made one, as it aligns with patterns seen in other zoonotic viruses.

The natural origin theory thus remains one of the leading explanations for the emergence of SARS-CoV-2, backed by genetic research and historical precedents in virology. This theory provides an important perspective on COVID-19's origins, pointing to the ways human interaction with wildlife and environmental disruption can create new pathways for diseases to emerge. While not without its critics and limitations, the natural origin theory continues to offer a scientific explanation grounded in established epidemiological understanding and genetic analysis.

The Wet Market Hypothesis and Early Transmission Theories

One of the earliest and most widely discussed theories about the origin of COVID-19 centers around the Huanan Seafood Wholesale Market in Wuhan, China. Known for its bustling environment and wide variety of live animals sold for food, the market initially drew suspicion as a possible starting point for the pandemic. When Chinese authorities first reported cases of a "pneumonia of unknown cause" in December 2019, many of the earliest infected individuals were found to have connections to this market, either as vendors or as frequent visitors. This raised concerns that COVID-19 might have originated from an animal source there, prompting scientists to consider the market a potential ground zero for the virus.

Wet markets, like the Huanan Market, are common in parts of Asia and other regions around the world. These markets bring together an array of live animals—fish, poultry, and wild animals like civets and pangolins—held in close quarters. While wet markets serve cultural and economic purposes, they also create conditions conducive to zoonotic transmission, where diseases can move from one species to another and, eventually, to humans. Pathogens can easily spread among animals kept in cages, as they are often in stressful conditions and close proximity, which weakens their immune systems and makes viral transmission more likely. When humans enter this environment, the likelihood of zoonotic spillover increases.

Initial investigations of the Huanan Market found traces of SARS-CoV-2 on surfaces throughout the market, leading to further speculation that the market was a focal point for viral transmission. Scientists and health authorities found viral particles on tables, door handles, and other surfaces, suggesting a widespread contamination. Additionally, the clustering of early COVID-19 cases among people associated with the market reinforced this theory. Although no direct evidence of a single "patient zero" at the market has been found, the epidemiological link was strong enough to prompt widespread investigation into the specific animals sold there. It was suggested that SARS-CoV-2 could have emerged from one or more animal species within the market, which may have acted as intermediary hosts between bats, believed to be the original reservoirs, and humans.

Efforts to identify the specific animal species responsible for transmitting the virus to humans have been challenging. Early testing of animals present at the market did not reveal direct evidence of SARS-CoV-2. As a result, researchers hypothesized that an intermediary animal—potentially a species that was not present during the investigations—might have initially carried the virus. Civet cats, which were implicated in the SARS outbreak of 2003, and pangolins, which carry coronaviruses similar to SARS-CoV-2, have been considered possible candidates. However, no definitive link has been established, leaving the precise animal pathway of COVID-19's jump to humans an open question.

The wet market hypothesis also sparked a global conversation about the role of wildlife trade in zoonotic diseases. Conservationists and scientists called for increased regulation and even the closure of certain types of wet markets to reduce the risk of future outbreaks. This push stems from concerns that close human-wildlife interactions in such markets make them breeding grounds for new diseases. Several countries responded by implementing stricter wildlife trade regulations or temporarily closing wet markets that sold live wild animals, with China instituting a ban on the sale and consumption of wild animals for food in early 2020. These actions, although significant, faced challenges in enforcement and cultural pushback, as such markets are deeply woven into local economies and traditions.

Despite these initial suspicions, further investigation revealed complexities that cast doubt on the Huanan Market's role as the primary origin of COVID-19. Subsequent studies indicated that some of the earliest cases in Wuhan had no connection to the market, suggesting that community transmission was already occurring in the city before the outbreak was linked to the market. These findings raised the possibility that the virus may have been circulating more widely before it was detected in December 2019, and that the market served as an amplifier for the spread rather than the original source.

The hypothesis that the Huanan Market was central to COVID-19's emergence is still a topic of active research and debate, highlighting the complex interplay between human behavior, animal trade, and zoonotic diseases. While the market hypothesis underscores how live animal markets can facilitate viral transmission, the true origin of SARS-CoV-2 remains unresolved. Nevertheless, this early focus on the market helped shape our understanding of the factors that may increase the risk of pandemics, encouraging scientists and policymakers to consider the need for more rigorous monitoring of human-animal interactions in these environments. The Huanan Market and other wet markets worldwide thus serve as cautionary symbols of the potential health risks tied to traditional practices, bringing new urgency to discussions on global health and disease prevention.

Genetic Analysis Supporting Natural Origin

The natural origin theory has found significant support in the field of genetic analysis, where scientists have scrutinized the structure of SARS-CoV-2 to understand its evolution and origins. By comparing SARS-CoV-2's genetic sequence with other known viruses, researchers have identified close similarities to coronaviruses found in animal species, especially bats and pangolins. This evidence strengthens the case that COVID-19 likely emerged through a natural zoonotic pathway rather than through human manipulation or a laboratory-based creation.

Genetic sequencing is a powerful tool in virology, allowing scientists to decode a virus's RNA and track its lineage. In early 2020, scientists sequenced the genome of SARS-CoV-2, which consists of roughly 30,000 RNA base pairs. By comparing this sequence to databases of known viruses, researchers found that SARS-CoV-2 shares approximately 96% of its genome with a bat coronavirus identified in Rhinolophus bats, a species commonly found in Asia. This close genetic match indicates that bats are likely the primary reservoir for the virus, supporting the idea that SARS-CoV-2 has a natural origin.

Further genetic analyses revealed similarities between SARS-CoV-2 and coronaviruses found in pangolins, a scaly mammal native to Asia and Africa that is sometimes trafficked for its meat and scales. Although pangolins are not considered the definitive intermediate host, some strains of coronaviruses found in pangolins share unique genetic features with SARS-CoV-2, particularly in the virus's spike protein. The spike protein, which binds to receptors on human cells, is critical in enabling the virus to infect its host. Finding similar spike proteins in animal coronaviruses strengthens the natural origin hypothesis, suggesting that SARS-CoV-2 could have acquired these genetic traits in an animal host, adapting over time to facilitate human infection.

One of the key arguments supporting a natural origin lies in SARS-CoV-2's receptor-binding domain (RBD), which is part of the spike protein responsible for attaching to human cells. Genetic studies have shown that the RBD of SARS-CoV-2 is highly effective at binding with ACE2 receptors on human cells, yet its structure does not display markers typically associated with artificial manipulation. In other words, the RBD of SARS-CoV-2 appears to have evolved naturally rather than being engineered in a laboratory. Computer models and molecular analyses have found that if scientists had attempted to design a virus optimized for human infection, they would likely have chosen a different structure than the one found in SARS-CoV-2. This "imperfect" structure actually makes the virus's natural evolution more plausible, as laboratory manipulation would likely leave identifiable genetic fingerprints that have not been observed.

Phylogenetic studies, which analyze the evolutionary relationships between different organisms, have also provided evidence in favor of natural origin. By constructing a phylogenetic tree, scientists can trace how SARS-CoV-2 is related to other viruses and estimate when they diverged from a common ancestor. Such studies suggest that SARS-CoV-2 is part of a larger family of coronaviruses that have been circulating in animal populations for years, possibly even decades. This finding is consistent with natural evolution, as viruses often circulate within animal reservoirs before undergoing mutations that enable them to infect humans.

Additionally, analysis of SARS-CoV-2's mutation patterns over time has supported the notion of natural evolution. As the virus spread globally, it accumulated mutations that scientists could track to understand how it adapted in different environments. This process, known as genetic drift, further suggests that SARS-CoV-2 evolved through natural selection rather than deliberate engineering. The absence of specific markers of human intervention, combined with SARS-CoV-2's natural mutation pattern, provides compelling evidence that the virus's evolution was shaped by ecological and biological forces rather than human intervention.

Nevertheless, the genetic similarity to bat and pangolin coronaviruses does not mean that scientists have identified the exact path SARS-CoV-2 took to reach humans. The search for a direct ancestor or intermediate host remains ongoing, with researchers examining wildlife species worldwide to pinpoint potential carriers. The lack of an exact match between SARS-CoV-2 and known animal viruses has left open questions and fueled alternative origin theories, but it is not uncommon in zoonotic research. Identifying the precise intermediate species involved in a zoonotic spillover event is often a lengthy and complex process, as seen with other diseases. Despite these challenges, the weight of genetic evidence points to natural processes as the most likely source of SARS-CoV-2.

The genetic analysis of SARS-CoV-2 thus serves as a foundation for understanding the origins of COVID-19, supporting the broader scientific consensus that the virus likely emerged through natural pathways rather than through human manipulation. This conclusion, drawn from genomic similarities with animal viruses and the absence of indicators of artificial engineering, aligns with historical patterns observed in other zoonotic diseases. While some mysteries remain regarding the specific pathway SARS-CoV-2 took to reach humans, the genetic evidence provides a compelling case for the natural origin theory, underscoring the interconnectedness of ecosystems and the potential for animal viruses to impact human health.

Evidence from Previous Zoonotic Outbreaks

Examining the history of zoonotic outbreaks provides valuable insight into how diseases like COVID-19 likely originated. Many past pandemics have emerged from animal reservoirs, underscoring the natural transmission pathways that enable animal-borne viruses to infect humans. Understanding these cases highlights the similarities between SARS-CoV-2 and previous zoonotic diseases, strengthening the theory that COVID-19 emerged through similar, natural channels.

One of the most notable zoonotic outbreaks in recent history was the 2003 SARS (Severe Acute Respiratory Syndrome) epidemic. Like COVID-19, SARS was caused by a coronavirus, SARS-CoV, which was traced back to an animal origin. SARS-CoV initially circulated in bats before making its way into humans through an intermediate host, the civet cat, a small mammal often found in Chinese wet markets. Scientists believe that civet cats, which can contract and spread the virus, acted as a bridge between bats and humans, allowing SARS-CoV to evolve and adapt to human hosts. This transmission pathway illustrates how coronaviruses can jump between species under natural conditions, especially in environments where humans and wild animals interact closely.

Another example is MERS (Middle East Respiratory Syndrome), a zoonotic disease caused by MERS-CoV, which emerged in Saudi Arabia in 2012. MERS is also a coronavirus, initially transmitted from bats to camels, which then passed the virus to humans. Camels are a significant part of life in many Middle Eastern cultures, and frequent contact between humans and camels likely facilitated the virus's transmission. Like SARS-CoV, MERS-CoV adapted in intermediate hosts, underscoring how viruses can gradually evolve to infect humans without any human intervention. MERS-CoV's journey from bats to camels and finally to humans supports the view that coronaviruses possess a natural ability to adapt across species, explaining how COVID-19 could have followed a similar path.

Beyond coronaviruses, other viruses with zoonotic origins, such as Ebola, Zika, and H5N1 avian flu, further demonstrate the potential for animal viruses to cause human outbreaks. The Ebola virus, first identified in 1976, is believed to reside in fruit bats. Multiple Ebola outbreaks have occurred when humans came into contact with infected animals, either through hunting, handling, or consuming bushmeat. Zika, which gained global attention in 2015-2016 due to its rapid spread and impact on fetal development, originated in primates and was transmitted to humans via mosquitoes. Similarly, the H5N1 avian flu virus, which primarily affects birds, has occasionally infected humans who had close contact with infected poultry. These examples underscore how various ecological factors, including close animal contact, can lead to the natural spillover of animal viruses into human populations.

Each of these cases offers a pattern consistent with SARS-CoV-2's suspected origin. Zoonotic spillover typically occurs when humans encroach on animal habitats, creating opportunities for viruses to cross species barriers. Globalization and population growth have led to increased interaction between humans and wildlife, intensifying the risk of zoonotic transmission. Deforestation, urban expansion, and the wildlife trade have all brought people closer to animal reservoirs, creating more frequent interactions that allow viruses to evolve and adapt to new hosts. The natural settings that fostered SARS-CoV and MERS-CoV transmissions also exist in the case of SARS-CoV-2, which likely spilled over in a context of close human-animal contact, similar to wet markets and wildlife interactions that have historically facilitated such transmissions.

In light of these historical outbreaks, the notion that SARS-CoV-2 could have emerged through a zoonotic spillover becomes more plausible. The pathways by which zoonotic diseases have traditionally spread reflect the natural processes of viral evolution. For scientists, these past outbreaks offer both a framework for understanding COVID-19 and a cautionary tale of how human activities can set the stage for pandemics. In many of these cases, initial animal-to-human transmission was followed by human-to-human spread, which allowed these viruses to spread widely and quickly, resulting in major public health crises. This pattern was also evident in the early stages of COVID-19, where initial cases linked to animal markets eventually gave way to widespread community transmission.

By studying these past zoonotic outbreaks, scientists have developed a strong understanding of how natural selection operates in viral evolution. Viruses like SARS-CoV-2 can mutate and adapt within animal hosts, gradually gaining traits that make them capable of infecting humans. Once a virus gains this capability, it can exploit human contact points, such as markets or farming environments, where multiple species, including humans, are present. In such environments, a virus with transmissible traits can quickly infect individuals who interact with the animal carriers, initiating the first step in a potential outbreak.

The parallels between SARS-CoV-2 and other zoonotic viruses reinforce the natural origin theory, suggesting that COVID-19's emergence followed an established pattern rather than an engineered one. While each virus has its unique characteristics, the historical trajectory of zoonotic diseases shares key commonalities, offering a broader understanding of how pathogens from the animal world can disrupt human society. This view emphasizes the importance of addressing ecological and environmental factors to mitigate future zoonotic outbreaks, as these factors frequently set the stage for disease spillover. As long as humans continue to interact with animal reservoirs, the risk of similar viruses emerging remains a critical consideration in global public health.

Counterarguments to the Lab-Origin Theory

The lab-origin theory, while widely speculated, encounters significant scientific, logistical, and historical counterarguments. Advocates for the natural origin theory assert that the evidence overwhelmingly favors a zoonotic spillover, rooted in patterns observed in previous pandemics and bolstered by rigorous genetic analysis of SARS-CoV-2. By examining the natural pathways through which similar viruses have emerged, researchers highlight the lack of substantive evidence linking COVID-19's origin to laboratory manipulation or mishandling. Additionally, experts emphasize the structural and functional characteristics of SARS-CoV-2, which point more toward evolution in animal hosts than to human design or laboratory modification.

One of the main counterpoints to the lab-origin hypothesis rests on genetic analysis. Many virologists argue that SARS-CoV-2's structure lacks the telltale signs of human engineering. Viruses manipulated in a laboratory often display specific genetic markers—mutations or arrangements that deviate from what is typically found in nature. In SARS-CoV-2, scientists have not observed these artificial modifications. For instance, the receptor-binding domain (RBD), which allows the virus to attach to human cells, does not display characteristics that suggest intentional engineering. Instead, the RBD appears to be a product of natural evolution, designed through trial and error across multiple generations in animal hosts, a process that has been observed in similar viruses. This evidence undermines the argument for a lab-based origin, as it indicates that SARS-CoV-2's structure developed through evolutionary processes rather than genetic modification.

Historical data from previous zoonotic outbreaks further challenges the lab-origin theory by establishing a pattern of natural spillover. Epidemics caused by viruses like SARS, MERS, Ebola, and H1N1 influenza all originated in animal reservoirs before adapting to infect humans. These viruses followed well-documented pathways from animal hosts to humans without requiring laboratory intervention. The consistent emergence of such zoonotic diseases suggests that COVID-19 likely followed a similar path. Given that wet markets and wildlife trafficking create high-risk environments for cross-species viral transmission, SARS-CoV-2 could have easily transitioned from animals to humans under natural conditions. By framing COVID-19 in this context, scientists argue that the virus's origin aligns more closely with past zoonotic events than with an unprecedented laboratory accident or release.

Logistical challenges also weaken the lab-origin theory. Many proponents of this theory suggest that SARS-CoV-2 might have been accidentally released due to a laboratory mishap. However, biosecurity protocols at high-level containment facilities, like the Wuhan Institute of Virology, are specifically designed to minimize the risk of accidental release. These facilities adhere to international safety standards that include rigorous containment measures, constant monitoring, and controlled access to dangerous pathogens. Though no security system is infallible, experts contend that the likelihood of an accidental release in a top-tier facility is very low, especially in light of the extensive protocols in place. This argument suggests that the lab-origin theory relies more on hypothetical possibilities than on concrete evidence of a breach or mishandling.

An additional counterargument is the lack of direct evidence linking SARS-CoV-2 to any laboratory. Investigations have not found documentation or records indicating that the Wuhan Institute of Virology was working with SARS-CoV-2 or a closely related virus before the pandemic. While the institute was indeed conducting research on coronaviruses, there is no documented proof that they possessed or modified a virus with the precise characteristics of SARS-CoV-2. Furthermore, scientists studying the virus's genome have not found a match to any known laboratory samples, making it unlikely that the virus was either engineered or accidentally released. Without a clear link between the virus and any specific lab, the theory remains speculative.

The lab-origin hypothesis also appears to have gained traction more through public skepticism and political discourse than through scientific support. Early in the pandemic, as COVID-19 spread globally, uncertainties surrounding the virus's origin fueled speculation, particularly in media and political circles. Public distrust toward Chinese transparency on COVID-19 reporting led some to assume a cover-up, further amplifying theories of a laboratory origin. However, scientific consensus largely supports the natural origin theory, based on genetic and epidemiological data. Political and social factors, rather than evidence-based findings, seem to drive the persistence of the lab-origin theory in public discussions. This discrepancy highlights the distinction between public perception and scientific evaluation.

In conclusion, these counterarguments collectively cast doubt on the plausibility of a lab-based origin for SARS-CoV-2. Genetic studies suggest that SARS-CoV-2's characteristics are consistent with natural viral evolution, while historical parallels emphasize that zoonotic outbreaks have repeatedly emerged from animal reservoirs without laboratory intervention. Stringent laboratory protocols make accidental release unlikely, and the lack of concrete evidence directly linking SARS-CoV-2 to any laboratory sample further weakens the theory. While questions surrounding COVID-19's origin remain, the scientific perspective leans strongly toward a natural spillover, grounded in empirical data and the patterns observed in previous zoonotic pandemics. As the search for definitive answers continues, these arguments emphasize the need to distinguish between hypothesis and evidence, ensuring that conclusions are based on factual analysis rather than speculation.

Chapter 6: Lab-Leak Theory

Overview of the Lab-Leak Theory

The lab-leak theory emerged as one of the earliest and most controversial explanations for the origin of COVID-19. This theory proposes that SARS-CoV-2, the virus responsible for the pandemic, may have accidentally escaped from a laboratory, specifically the Wuhan Institute of Virology (WIV) in Wuhan, China—the very city where the first known COVID-19 cases were reported. As scientists and the public alike grappled with the sudden global spread of the virus, the lab-leak theory quickly gained traction, fueled by a combination of scientific curiosity, political tension, and public fear.

In the early days of the pandemic, researchers rushed to determine how SARS-CoV-2 might have crossed over from animals to humans. Initial theories pointed to zoonotic spillover, similar to previous coronaviruses such as SARS and MERS, which had jumped from animals to humans through intermediate hosts. However, as the search for a definitive animal source yielded no conclusive results, alternative theories began to emerge. The idea that the virus could have originated in a lab, rather than through a direct animal-to-human transfer, took root, and questions surrounding WIV became central to this hypothesis. The institute was known to conduct research on coronaviruses, including studies on bat coronaviruses closely related to SARS-CoV-2, which raised concerns among those skeptical of the natural-origin hypothesis.

The lab-leak theory posits that WIV, a high-security research facility specializing in virology, could have inadvertently released SARS-CoV-2 into the community. Some proponents of this theory pointed to potential lapses in safety protocols, arguing that despite WIV's classification as a Biosafety Level 4 (BSL-4) facility, even the most stringent protocols cannot entirely eliminate the risk of accidental release. They also emphasized the institute's proximity to the outbreak's initial cluster of cases, citing it as more than a coincidence. The theory further gained credibility due to the nature of research conducted at WIV, particularly studies involving "gain-of-function" techniques. These techniques, which are used to enhance the infectiousness or virulence of a pathogen for research purposes, raised questions about the possibility that a laboratory-modified virus could have escaped into the human population.

Public and scientific interest in the lab-leak theory was intensified by reports that WIV staff had experienced flu-like symptoms shortly before the official outbreak, as well as accounts that certain records and data from the institute were restricted or removed from public access. These reports, combined with the Chinese government's initial lack of transparency in sharing data and virus samples, led to widespread speculation and suspicion. As a result, the lab-leak theory gained traction not only among scientists but also among journalists, politicians, and the general public.

In examining how the lab-leak theory gained prominence, it's crucial to consider the voices of its early proponents. Among them were several high-profile scientists, investigative journalists, and government officials who called for an impartial, transparent inquiry into COVID-19's origins. This chorus included figures who felt that China's response to early inquiries was uncooperative or evasive, raising concerns about what might be concealed from global scrutiny. As the pandemic unfolded, international pressure mounted on China to provide greater transparency, with calls for an independent investigation into WIV and its practices. The lab-leak theory became a focal point for debates on global health accountability, laboratory safety, and the need for transparent scientific inquiry.

As the theory spread, it faced opposition and support alike, with scientists divided over its plausibility. While some researchers stressed the lack of direct evidence linking SARS-CoV-2 to WIV, others argued that the absence of a clear zoonotic source and the circumstantial proximity of WIV to the outbreak warranted further investigation. This ongoing debate underscored both the theory's complexity and the difficulty of reaching consensus amid a crisis.

In summary, the lab-leak theory evolved from a fringe hypothesis to a central narrative of the COVID-19 origin debate. It brought the Wuhan Institute of Virology into the spotlight, raising questions about research ethics, lab safety, and the international response to emerging pathogens. Whether ultimately proven or not, the theory underscored the need for greater transparency and global cooperation in understanding and preventing future pandemics. As investigations into COVID-19's origins continue, the lab-leak theory remains an important facet of the broader conversation surrounding the pandemic and its impact on global public health policies.

Key Proponents and Arguments for the Lab-Leak Theory

The lab-leak theory attracted significant support from a range of proponents who raised questions about COVID-19's origins, largely centered on concerns over lab safety and research practices at the Wuhan Institute of Virology (WIV). Early advocates of the theory included scientists, investigative journalists, and government officials, all of whom cited various factors that seemed, at the very least, circumstantial, yet too notable to ignore. These figures brought the theory into the public eye, arguing that the combination of geographical proximity, research practices at WIV, and alleged lapses in transparency made a compelling case for deeper investigation.

Among the prominent voices advocating for a closer look at the lab-leak theory was Dr. Richard Ebright, a molecular biologist and biosafety expert who expressed concerns over gain-of-function research—scientific studies that involve altering viruses to assess their potential to cause pandemics. For Ebright and others, the idea that a highly contagious virus could be accidentally released from a lab conducting such risky experiments was not far-fetched. They pointed out that WIV had previously conducted gain-of-function research on bat coronaviruses similar to SARS-CoV-2. This fact, proponents argued, was an indicator that SARS-CoV-2 could have originated from a similar study gone wrong, rather than from a natural zoonotic jump.

Another group of proponents included investigative journalists, whose work brought attention to circumstantial evidence supporting the lab-leak theory. For instance, journalists noted reports suggesting that WIV researchers may have fallen ill with symptoms resembling COVID-19 in the weeks leading up to the official outbreak. While these reports remained unconfirmed, they fueled suspicions and suggested that the timeline of the virus's spread could be different from what was initially believed. Journalists also highlighted inconsistencies in the Chinese government's communication with international health organizations, particularly in the early stages of the outbreak. Some argued that these inconsistencies indicated an attempt to control the narrative surrounding the virus's origin, which in turn raised suspicions about WIV's possible role.

Government officials, particularly in the United States, also became strong advocates for the lab-leak theory. Figures such as then-Secretary of State Mike Pompeo openly questioned the transparency of the Chinese government and the World Health Organization (WHO) in disclosing information about the virus's origins. For these officials, the close geographic link between WIV and the outbreak's epicenter seemed to indicate more than a coincidence. They pointed to China's reluctance to allow independent investigators full access to WIV and its records as a potential red flag. These officials argued that without unfettered access, the possibility of a lab accident could not be fully ruled out and warranted further investigation.

The proponents also highlighted what they saw as gaps in the zoonotic origin theory, arguing that while zoonotic spillovers were common, they generally left clear trails that scientists could follow. In the case of SARS-CoV-2, however, researchers had yet to find an intermediate host, such as a civet cat or camel, which could have carried the virus from bats to humans. This absence, proponents claimed, raised questions about whether the virus had in fact followed a natural evolutionary path. For many lab-leak advocates, the inability to conclusively link SARS-CoV-2 to a specific animal host made a lab origin more plausible.

These arguments were bolstered by reports from U.S. intelligence, which suggested that certain records at WIV may have been altered or removed from public access shortly after the outbreak began. Proponents viewed these actions as potentially suspicious and indicative of an effort to prevent scrutiny of WIV's research activities. Although no direct evidence of a cover-up emerged, lab-leak proponents argued that the removal of access to records deserved further examination. The theory gained further traction when high-profile scientists, including Nobel laureates, joined the call for a more thorough investigation, adding scientific legitimacy to the discussion.

In sum, advocates for the lab-leak theory built their case on a combination of circumstantial evidence, historical precedent, and perceived irregularities in the behavior of WIV and the Chinese government. For these proponents, the question was not about proving a definitive lab origin, but rather ensuring that all plausible explanations were thoroughly explored. They argued that the stakes were too high to dismiss the lab-leak theory without a transparent, independent investigation, and they called for international pressure to ensure accountability in scientific research practices.

Evidence and Arguments Supporting the Lab-Leak Theory

The lab-leak theory, though controversial, rests on several key pieces of circumstantial evidence and scientific arguments that, while not definitive, suggest the theory deserves serious consideration. Proponents of the lab-leak theory highlight specific data points and patterns that raise questions about whether SARS-CoV-2 could have accidentally escaped from the Wuhan Institute of Virology (WIV), rather than emerging through natural transmission. They argue that these details, while not direct proof, collectively point to a plausible scenario that warrants further investigation. This section examines the main evidence and arguments supporting the lab-leak hypothesis.

One of the most discussed points of evidence relates to the virus's initial outbreak location. Wuhan, the city where COVID-19 first emerged, is also home to WIV, which has long been a hub for coronavirus research. Scientists at WIV had been studying bat coronaviruses similar to SARS-CoV-2, some of which were acquired from remote caves in China known to harbor high-risk pathogens. Lab-leak theory supporters argue that the coincidence of the outbreak occurring in Wuhan, home to a major virology lab with a history of working on similar viruses, is too close to ignore. To them, it suggests that the virus may have originated within the lab and inadvertently spread to the surrounding community.

Another key component of the lab-leak argument concerns the virus's unique genetic features. Some proponents point to the presence of a particular trait known as the "furin cleavage site" in SARS-CoV-2. This site, which enhances the virus's ability to infect human cells, is absent in many related coronaviruses and appears to be a significant factor in the virus's high transmissibility. The furin cleavage site is unusual enough that it has led some virologists to question whether it could have been naturally acquired or whether it might have been the result of laboratory manipulation. While gain-of-function research—experiments designed to enhance the infectivity of a virus—is intended to prepare for potential pandemics, lab-leak proponents argue that it could also lead to accidental releases of enhanced pathogens. The existence of the furin cleavage site has thus fueled speculation that SARS-CoV-2 could have been altered or studied in a laboratory setting before being unintentionally released.

The timing of the outbreak has also raised questions. According to some reports, WIV researchers fell ill with COVID-like symptoms in the months leading up to the officially recognized start of the pandemic. Although these reports remain unconfirmed and are based on limited intelligence, they suggest that COVID-19 may have been circulating in the vicinity of WIV prior to the first reported cases. For lab-leak proponents, this information supports the theory of a potential lab origin, as it hints that the virus may have escaped before health authorities were alerted to its presence.

A significant part of the lab-leak argument also lies in the practices at WIV and other laboratories worldwide regarding biosafety protocols. Although WIV is a high-security lab classified as Biosafety Level 4 (BSL-4), it has also conducted virus research in lower-level Biosafety Level 2 (BSL-2) labs. BSL-2 is not equipped to handle the most dangerous pathogens, as it lacks the stringent containment measures of a BSL-4 facility. Given that coronaviruses similar to SARS-CoV-2 were reportedly handled in these less secure environments, lab-leak proponents argue that the chance of accidental release was higher than it would have been under stricter containment. Safety concerns are not new in the field of virology, as history has documented multiple cases of laboratory-acquired infections and accidental releases, even in highly regulated settings. Thus, advocates of the lab-leak theory suggest that WIV's handling of high-risk viruses in a less secure setting could have inadvertently contributed to a leak.

Another line of evidence that lab-leak proponents highlight is the lack of an intermediate host. In past zoonotic outbreaks, scientists have typically identified an intermediary species that facilitated the virus's transmission from animals to humans, as seen with SARS in 2002-2003, where civet cats were eventually identified as the intermediary. However, despite extensive testing and studies, scientists have yet to find an intermediate animal host for SARS-CoV-2, which lab-leak advocates argue is suspicious. They assert that if SARS-CoV-2 had a natural origin, an animal host would likely have been identified by now, given the scale and depth of testing efforts around the world.

In summary, the lab-leak theory is supported by a combination of geographic coincidence, genetic features, reports of early infections, biosafety practices at WIV, and the ongoing absence of a confirmed intermediate host. Each of these elements, on its own, is not conclusive proof of a laboratory origin. However, together, they form a basis for legitimate inquiry and further investigation. Proponents argue that these pieces of evidence underscore the need for transparent, independent research into COVID-19's origins to either confirm or dispel the lab-leak hypothesis. While the evidence remains circumstantial, it has been compelling enough to keep the lab-leak theory a central and ongoing part of the COVID-19 origin debate.

Counterpoints to the Lab-Leak Theory

As the lab-leak theory gained traction, many scientists and experts presented counterarguments to challenge its plausibility, arguing that the evidence supporting a natural origin is more consistent with known patterns of viral evolution. These counterpoints focus on the lack of direct evidence for a laboratory release, as well as on established scientific principles regarding zoonotic spillover events. Critics of the lab-leak theory argue that while coincidences such as the Wuhan Institute of Virology's proximity to the outbreak may appear suspicious, they are not enough to substantiate claims of a laboratory origin. Instead, they suggest that the virus's characteristics align more closely with natural evolution and transmission processes, rather than with the traits one might expect from a virus engineered or released from a lab.

One of the primary counterpoints centers around the evolutionary characteristics of SARS-CoV-2. Opponents of the lab-leak theory argue that the virus's genetic structure does not exhibit clear hallmarks of laboratory manipulation. Specifically, many researchers have pointed to the absence of any genetic "fingerprint" that would indicate intentional engineering. The argument here is that if SARS-CoV-2 had been engineered, especially as part of gain-of-function research, it would likely show signs of direct human intervention at the molecular level. However, SARS-CoV-2's genetic sequence does not carry identifiable markers of such tampering, suggesting instead that its unique characteristics likely developed through natural selection. Some studies have shown that the virus's closest known relatives in bats and other species indicate a path of evolution that could have led to the virus's adaptation to humans without the need for lab intervention.

Another counterpoint concerns the viability of zoonotic spillover, which remains a well-documented route for infectious diseases. Critics argue that the world has seen numerous instances of zoonotic diseases emerging without any lab involvement, as in the case of HIV, Ebola, and other coronaviruses like SARS and MERS. These zoonotic transmissions are natural processes by which viruses adapt to human hosts. For these critics, the rapid spread of SARS-CoV-2 resembles previous pandemics in which viruses jumped from animals to humans in environments where humans and wildlife closely interacted. Wet markets, including those in Wuhan, are often densely populated and feature diverse species in close quarters, creating an environment where zoonotic spillover is more likely to occur. Critics contend that SARS-CoV-2's appearance in such a setting is far from unprecedented and does not require lab involvement as an explanation.

Additionally, the international scientific community has conducted multiple investigations and analyses into the virus's origins, including some led by the World Health Organization (WHO). While the WHO's initial investigation faced criticism for limited access to data, it concluded that a natural zoonotic origin was "likely to very likely," while describing a lab-related origin as "extremely unlikely." Despite calls for further transparency and concerns over China's handling of the investigation, scientists have reiterated that zoonotic transmission remains the most plausible origin pathway. Critics of the lab-leak theory suggest that focusing on a lab-based explanation may detract from crucial epidemiological and ecological research aimed at preventing future zoonotic outbreaks. They argue that continued investigation into wildlife markets, animal carriers, and ecological factors will provide more actionable insights into how these viruses emerge.

The counterargument also addresses the issue of biosafety. Although some lab-leak proponents highlight concerns over WIV's biosafety protocols, particularly in BSL-2 labs, critics argue that similar research on bat coronaviruses is conducted in labs around the world under similar biosafety levels. These biosafety levels are standardized globally, meaning that WIV's practices were consistent with those of other major research institutions. Moreover, they argue that an accident involving a virus as transmissible as SARS-CoV-2 would likely leave a clear trail of infection among laboratory staff, yet no such evidence has been definitively established. For many scientists, the absence of any confirmed early cases among WIV staff is a significant counterpoint, as a lab-acquired infection would likely have been easier to trace back to its origins.

Lastly, counterarguments address the challenges of proving a negative. Detractors of the lab-leak theory argue that proving the non-involvement of a laboratory is inherently difficult, especially when much of the discussion revolves around circumstantial evidence rather than direct proof. Some scientists believe that continued focus on the lab-leak theory risks overlooking the importance of transparent scientific collaboration. They argue that in the absence of concrete evidence linking SARS-CoV-2 to a lab, the more productive approach is to focus on well-supported theories of zoonotic origin. This approach, they contend, aligns with established scientific methodologies that prioritize evidence-based conclusions over speculative connections.

In conclusion, while the lab-leak theory remains a topic of serious debate, numerous counterarguments underscore the plausibility of a natural origin. By focusing on genetic indicators, historical patterns of zoonotic transmission, international investigations, and the realities of biosafety protocols, critics of the lab-leak theory argue that SARS-CoV-2 most likely emerged through natural processes. These counterpoints highlight that, although the lab-leak theory raises valid questions, it lacks the conclusive evidence needed to supplant the natural origin theory, which remains widely regarded by the scientific community as the most probable explanation for the origins of COVID-19.

Balancing Scientific Objectivity with Public Curiosity

The debate over the origins of COVID-19 has highlighted a challenging intersection between scientific rigor and public curiosity. On one side, the scientific community is dedicated to following evidence-based methods, carefully analyzing data before drawing conclusions. On the other, the general public has become increasingly invested in understanding the origins of the pandemic, fueled by personal losses, economic hardship, and a desire for accountability. In navigating these two spheres, the discourse surrounding the lab-leak theory and the natural origin hypothesis has become emblematic of a larger conversation: how to balance the methodical pace of science with the public's demand for transparency and rapid answers.

The scientific method is structured to produce reliable knowledge, but it is also inherently slow. Research is often an iterative process involving hypothesis testing, peer review, and gradual accumulation of evidence. This process stands in stark contrast to the fast-paced environment of news media, where speculative theories can quickly take root and spread widely, often without the rigorous scrutiny scientists apply to research findings. As a result, the public can sometimes receive fragmented or incomplete views of scientific progress, particularly when discussions involve complex fields like virology and epidemiology. In the case of COVID-19's origins, early theories and inconclusive data have often been presented as definitive findings, blurring the lines between confirmed science and hypothesis.

Public interest in the lab-leak theory, in particular, has been driven in part by the accountability factor. With the pandemic's massive impact on global health and economies, many people feel that understanding the virus's origins could potentially prevent future pandemics and hold those responsible accountable if negligence or missteps contributed to its spread. Public figures, including politicians, have seized on these concerns to press for transparency and additional investigations, adding a political dimension to the scientific debate. While public demand for answers is entirely understandable, the pressure to arrive at a "satisfying" explanation can sometimes encourage premature conclusions. Scientists, meanwhile, emphasize that transparency should not compromise scientific integrity, as drawing conclusions without definitive proof can lead to misinformation or misplaced blame.

Transparency, however, is essential to maintaining public trust, especially during a crisis as significant as the COVID-19 pandemic. The credibility of scientific institutions depends on their openness to scrutiny and accountability. Yet, the lab-leak theory debate has also demonstrated the limits of transparency, particularly in countries where information sharing is restricted or tightly controlled.

The Chinese government's handling of early COVID-19 data and its restricted access to Wuhan Institute of Virology records has raised questions about potential concealment, prompting calls for greater openness in international collaborations. Scientists argue that understanding COVID-19's origins would benefit immensely from unimpeded access to data, which would enable the global scientific community to conduct independent investigations that meet the rigorous standards of evidence-based research.

Balancing this need for scientific transparency with national and institutional sensitivities is challenging. In many ways, the COVID-19 origin debate underscores the necessity for enhanced global scientific cooperation and improved systems for sharing information about infectious disease research. Initiatives such as the WHO's Global Outbreak Alert and Response Network (GOARN) represent steps toward a unified, transparent approach to investigating and managing future pandemics. Still, more robust international agreements on data sharing, biosafety, and research transparency could facilitate quicker and more accurate responses when future outbreaks occur. Without such agreements, the gaps in transparency witnessed during the COVID-19 pandemic are likely to persist, with similar debates and tensions arising in the face of future health crises.

The widespread speculation surrounding COVID-19's origins has also sparked a broader conversation about the ethical responsibilities of scientists and research institutions. Some have suggested that more rigorous ethical guidelines and safety protocols should govern the study of highly infectious pathogens, especially when conducted in densely populated areas. This view emphasizes the ethical responsibility to prevent possible lab accidents or breaches that could harm the public, underscoring the need for clear, enforceable standards in the handling of dangerous pathogens. Institutions worldwide are beginning to assess and refine biosafety practices, particularly concerning gain-of-function research, which some believe may carry risks that outweigh the potential benefits.

In summary, the debate over COVID-19's origins illustrates the delicate balance between scientific rigor and public curiosity. It calls attention to the role of transparency in fostering public trust, the challenges of international cooperation, and the ethical responsibilities tied to research on dangerous pathogens. While the question of whether COVID-19 emerged naturally or as the result of a lab leak remains unresolved, the dialogue it has sparked underscores the need for improved communication between scientists, public institutions, and the general public. As new evidence comes to light, maintaining this balance will be essential for fostering a well-informed public and ensuring that scientific research is conducted in ways that prioritize both accuracy and safety.

Chapter 7: Political Implications and Reactions

Initial Political Responses to the Lab-Leak Theory

As the world grappled with the shocking emergence of COVID-19, theories about the virus's origin quickly became a lightning rod for political debate. Among these, the "lab-leak" theory—that the virus had accidentally escaped from a laboratory in Wuhan—seemed particularly charged. Early in 2020, scientific, governmental, and media circles began quietly circulating this notion, and as it reached the public, the theory took on a life of its own, fueling tension among nations, particularly between the U.S. and China. From the outset, global leaders and institutions found themselves navigating uncharted waters, balancing diplomacy with demands for transparency, all while trying to make sense of a rapidly escalating crisis.

When news first broke about a novel coronavirus in Wuhan, China's official response was swift but measured. Chinese officials reported that the initial cases were linked to the Huanan Seafood Wholesale Market, suggesting a zoonotic transmission—the idea that the virus jumped from animals to humans, similar to previous outbreaks like SARS. As the virus spread, China began implementing strict lockdown measures and publicly sharing genetic data of the virus with the international scientific community. At the time, this transparency was generally praised by global health organizations and many world leaders as a model of quick and effective crisis response.

However, as COVID-19 cases surged worldwide, whispers of a more complex narrative began to surface. Several scientists and analysts noticed that the Wuhan Institute of Virology (WIV), one of China's prominent research facilities for coronaviruses, was located a mere miles from the initial outbreak. The institute's proximity to the epicenter, coupled with ongoing research on bat coronaviruses, sparked early suspicions. Initially, these concerns remained largely speculative and were treated cautiously by most governments, particularly as the World Health Organization (WHO) publicly supported the zoonotic transmission theory. Yet, doubts lingered, prompting some officials, notably in the U.S., to call for a closer examination of the WIV.

In March 2020, the lab-leak theory gained traction in the United States, where high-ranking officials expressed unease over China's handling of the pandemic and the WHO's reliance on Chinese data. Secretary of State Mike Pompeo and President Donald Trump were among the first major political figures to publicly endorse the possibility that the virus could have originated in a laboratory. Their stance was not without consequence; calls for an investigation quickly became interwoven with existing trade tensions, and accusations of a lack of transparency were met with rebuttals from Beijing. As the U.S. position on the lab-leak theory became more assertive, a diplomatic rift grew between the two superpowers.

China's response was both defensive and defiant. Chinese officials and state media dismissed the lab-leak theory as baseless and anti-China propaganda, framing it as an attempt by the U.S. to shift blame for its own struggles to contain the virus. They argued that focusing on the lab-leak theory detracted from meaningful international cooperation needed to fight the pandemic. Further, they contended that such accusations fueled xenophobia, inciting distrust in the global community and complicating efforts to collaboratively develop a pandemic response.

As the lab-leak theory became a focal point of international discourse, the WHO faced mounting pressure to mediate and investigate. However, the organization's options were limited. By April 2020, the WHO announced its intention to send a team to China to investigate the origins of COVID-19. Yet their efforts were hampered by strict conditions imposed by Chinese authorities, including limitations on what data could be accessed and restrictions on visiting key locations, including the WIV. These restrictions, coupled with WHO's close reliance on data provided by Chinese scientists, drew criticism from several countries, particularly the U.S., who accused the organization of being unduly influenced by China. Meanwhile, China argued that the investigation was politically motivated, emphasizing that any research into COVID-19's origins should be scientific, not political.

By the summer of 2020, international lines were starkly drawn. Governments were either quietly supporting China's assertion of zoonotic transmission or voicing support for the lab-leak theory. European nations largely maintained a cautious approach, wary of straining economic ties with China while increasingly acknowledging the need for greater transparency. Other countries, particularly those with close alliances to the U.S., found themselves aligning with calls for a thorough and independent investigation, reinforcing an emerging geopolitical divide over COVID-19's origins.

As more countries voiced the need for an impartial inquiry, Australia became one of the first to formally call for an independent investigation, independent of the WHO. This move prompted swift backlash from China, who saw Australia's stance as an echo of U.S. rhetoric. Trade tensions between the two countries quickly escalated, with China imposing tariffs and restrictions on Australian imports, a move widely interpreted as economic retaliation. Australia's appeal for a probe became a powerful example of how a scientific inquiry into a virus's origin could quickly mutate into a point of contention with far-reaching economic and diplomatic consequences.

Thus, the lab-leak theory quickly transformed from a scientific inquiry into a symbol of international power struggles and political posturing. What began as a health crisis had escalated into a diplomatic standoff, with governments around the world taking sides, making statements, and enacting policies with implications that extended far beyond the lab in Wuhan. Scientific investigation became secondary to the political machinations at play, as countries grappled with how to respond not only to the virus itself but also to the complex landscape of international relations it had exposed.

This initial round of responses to the lab-leak theory set the stage for what would become an enduring battle of narratives. The world had entered a precarious dance, where scientific inquiry and geopolitical rivalry were intertwined, shaping both public opinion and international alliances. As the pandemic continued to unfold, the lab-leak theory would remain a contentious issue, one that laid bare the fault lines between scientific transparency, political maneuvering, and the urgent need for truth in a time of crisis.

Heightened Tensions Between the U.S. and China

As speculation over COVID-19's origins intensified, diplomatic relations between the United States and China grew increasingly strained. The virus had already disrupted global stability, affecting economies, healthcare systems, and the day-to-day lives of billions, but the questions surrounding where and how it began soon led to one of the most pronounced diplomatic standoffs of the 21st century. What had begun as a health crisis was rapidly evolving into a fierce geopolitical confrontation, with accusations and counter-accusations adding fuel to an already simmering rivalry.

The U.S. government, led by then-President Donald Trump, was vocal in its skepticism toward China's handling of the pandemic and its perceived lack of transparency. Early in the pandemic, American intelligence agencies were tasked with investigating the origins of COVID-19. Initial reports from these agencies were inconclusive, but some within the administration, including Secretary of State Mike Pompeo, argued that there was credible evidence suggesting the virus could have leaked from the Wuhan Institute of Virology (WIV). This hypothesis, while unconfirmed, aligned with broader concerns about China's transparency in managing the crisis.

Publicly, the Trump administration demanded that China provide more open access to data, research, and evidence regarding the early days of the outbreak. Their calls became increasingly urgent as the virus tore through the U.S., impacting every state and pushing the American healthcare system to its limits. In April 2020, President Trump openly suggested that COVID-19 could be a result of a laboratory mishap, accusing China of concealing crucial information. His administration's rhetoric was at times confrontational, painting China as a negligent, if not culpable, party in the global catastrophe.

China's response was swift and defensive. Chinese officials condemned the allegations as baseless and politically motivated, arguing that the U.S. was attempting to deflect attention from its own struggles to contain the virus. State media in China called the lab-leak theory a "smokescreen" to distract from American mismanagement of the pandemic. Chinese Foreign Ministry spokespeople further argued that China's response had been timely and transparent, pointing to the early genetic sequencing of the virus that China had shared with the world in January 2020, which had helped speed the development of diagnostic tools.

Amid the escalating rhetoric, China launched a counter-campaign, asserting that the virus could have originated outside of China. Chinese officials alluded to theories that COVID-19 might have been introduced to Wuhan via imported frozen food or even by the U.S. military during the Military World Games held in Wuhan in October 2019. These theories, although lacking scientific support, resonated with some in China and other parts of the world, reframing the narrative and deflecting blame from Beijing.

The political strain was not confined to rhetoric alone; it quickly impacted trade and international relations. As the U.S. pursued its investigation into the origins of COVID-19, China retaliated with economic measures, slowing down exports of medical supplies to the U.S. at a time when they were desperately needed. Although both countries were heavily dependent on each other economically, the tensions over COVID-19 exacerbated the ongoing trade war, leading to further tariffs, trade restrictions, and obstacles for multinational businesses operating in both nations.

Meanwhile, the world looked on, observing the standoff between two superpowers with growing concern. Leaders in Europe, Asia, and other parts of the world felt pressured to choose sides. For many countries, balancing their economic and political ties with both the

U.S. and China was already challenging, and the pandemic made it even more so. The European Union initially hesitated to support the lab-leak theory outright, focusing instead on calls for a global inquiry that could reveal more about the origins of the virus without assigning blame. However, the pressure from both Washington and Beijing made neutrality increasingly difficult to maintain.

Australia became one of the first countries to support the U.S. call for an independent inquiry into the origins of COVID-19. In April 2020, Prime Minister Scott Morrison called for a probe that would include investigations into the Wuhan Institute of Virology, a move that aligned with U.S. interests but angered China. Almost immediately, China responded with a series of trade sanctions, targeting key Australian exports such as barley, beef, and wine. China's response sent a message to other nations considering similar moves: supporting the lab-leak theory could come at an economic cost.

In Washington, policymakers saw this as a further indication of China's lack of transparency. For China, however, these actions were perceived as necessary measures to counter what they viewed as an attack on their sovereignty. Beijing argued that the U.S. was using the pandemic as a pretext to undermine China's rising global influence and economic power, intensifying an already complex rivalry.

The effects of this diplomatic struggle trickled down to the global scientific community. Scientists worldwide, many of whom relied on collaborations with Chinese researchers and access to Chinese data, found themselves caught between the demands of their governments and the pursuit of objective, independent research. The U.S.-China tensions created an environment where data sharing was restricted, and open collaboration was stifled. Researchers reported difficulties accessing samples, information, and datasets that could provide insight into the virus's origin, a setback that hampered global scientific efforts.

As the months wore on, the lab-leak theory continued to be a divisive issue, not only in government halls but also within academia, international organizations, and the media. The polarization over COVID-19's origins became emblematic of a larger geopolitical rift that would shape the course of global diplomacy long after the pandemic subsided. Governments, scientists, and citizens were left grappling with a crisis that was not merely a public health emergency but a geopolitical flashpoint that exposed the fragility of international cooperation.

The heightened U.S.-China tensions underscored the complexity of unraveling the origins of COVID-19. It became evident that, for better or worse, the question of the virus's origin was now inseparable from global politics. Where science and diplomacy might once have converged to find common ground, they were now strained by competing national interests and deep-seated mistrust. In this charged environment, the search for truth became not only a scientific quest but a political battleground that would shape the narratives, policies, and alliances of the post-pandemic world.

WHO and International Efforts for an Unbiased Investigation

In the midst of escalating international pressure to determine the origins of COVID-19, the World Health Organization (WHO) was thrust into a complex role, caught between the need for scientific objectivity and the growing political interests surrounding the pandemic's origin. In May 2020, under global scrutiny, the WHO announced it would lead an international investigation into the early days of the pandemic and the virus's possible origins. The organization's mission was to be impartial, driven by scientific inquiry, and independent from any national agendas—a formidable task given the geopolitical undercurrents that had already shaped the discourse.

At the request of member nations, the WHO assembled a team of international experts, including epidemiologists, virologists, and other specialists from around the world, with the hope of conducting a comprehensive investigation in China. The team was tasked with reviewing early cases, studying the virus's evolution, and understanding any factors that might have contributed to its emergence. The WHO planned to work alongside Chinese scientists and review crucial data from Wuhan, particularly from the Huanan Seafood Wholesale Market, where early cases were identified, as well as from the Wuhan Institute of Virology (WIV), which had attracted suspicion due to its research on coronaviruses.

The WHO investigation, however, faced a multitude of challenges even before it began. Negotiations between the WHO and Chinese authorities over the scope and access of the investigation stretched out over months. Chinese officials were wary of an inquiry that could potentially cast blame on their country, especially if the investigation suggested a failure of early containment or laboratory safety protocols. The Chinese government, while agreeing to cooperate with the WHO, insisted on stringent guidelines that would limit some aspects of the investigation, particularly access to raw data and certain facilities.

When the WHO team finally arrived in Wuhan in January 2021—more than a year after the pandemic's initial outbreak—scientific and political expectations were high. The world hoped for answers, or at the very least, clearer insight into how this virus might have emerged. As the team began its work, they found that many potential leads and early clues had been lost to time. Hospitals, laboratories, and markets had been thoroughly cleaned, and some records were no longer available. Interviews with patients, market workers, and lab personnel provided limited information, often constrained by both language barriers and the nervousness of being associated with the pandemic's origins.

The investigation included visits to the Huanan Seafood Market, the Wuhan Center for Disease Control, and the Wuhan Institute of Virology. However, the limited access became a source of frustration for many team members. The WHO experts were provided data by Chinese researchers but were not granted direct access to some of the raw case data and early samples that could have provided a clearer picture of COVID-19's early spread. Despite their best efforts, the WHO team's access to critical pieces of information remained filtered and incomplete, and the inability to access certain laboratory records led to lingering doubts over the credibility of the investigation's findings.

After weeks of research, the WHO team released its initial findings in March 2021. The report laid out several potential scenarios for the virus's origin, with the most likely hypothesis being zoonotic transmission—from animals to humans—potentially involving an intermediate species. The lab-leak theory, while not dismissed, was labeled as "extremely unlikely," a conclusion that drew mixed reactions. While some countries, including China, were quick to embrace the findings, others, particularly the United States, questioned the credibility of the report. Critics argued that the WHO's restricted access, combined with the political sensitivities at play, had limited the team's ability to conduct a truly independent investigation.

Public opinion over the WHO's report was polarized. Many saw it as a reasonable assessment based on available evidence, while others perceived it as an incomplete account influenced by political constraints. Several scientists, including members of the WHO team, voiced their concerns publicly, calling for further investigation and access to data that had remained off-limits. The debate over the report's findings intensified as governments, media outlets, and scientific bodies weighed in on its conclusions.

In response to the outcry, the WHO emphasized that its report was not definitive but rather a stepping stone for future research. Dr. Tedros Adhanom Ghebreyesus, the Director-General of the WHO, called for continued inquiry into the origins of COVID-19, stressing the need for full transparency and access to data, and implicitly acknowledging the limitations of the initial investigation. He urged China and other member states to support the next phase of the inquiry, expressing hope that further studies could address the remaining questions and foster greater international cooperation.

Despite the WHO's call for a follow-up investigation, the political barriers remained formidable. China insisted that the investigation should shift its focus to other countries, contending that the virus might have emerged elsewhere before being detected in Wuhan. This suggestion sparked diplomatic resistance from the United States and its allies, who argued that a comprehensive investigation in China was still crucial to understanding the full picture. The standoff became emblematic of the broader geopolitical struggle, as both Western nations and China sought to shape the narrative surrounding COVID-19's origins.

Meanwhile, calls for transparency grew louder within the scientific community, with prominent researchers and institutions joining the push for open data and international collaboration. Over a thousand scientists from multiple countries signed petitions, published open letters, and urged their governments to support unrestricted investigation efforts. Their appeals highlighted the need for science to transcend political divides, emphasizing that understanding COVID-19's origins was not merely a question of accountability but a necessary step to prevent future pandemics.

The WHO investigation ultimately underscored the difficulties inherent in conducting a transparent, unbiased inquiry amid political tensions. It revealed that, while science strives for objectivity, it often exists within a web of national interests and ideological divides. As the world debated the origins of COVID-19, the investigation served as a reminder of the challenges facing global health organizations in an era where science, politics, and public perception are deeply intertwined. The quest to unravel the truth about COVID-19's beginnings had become, in essence, a diplomatic minefield, testing the resilience of international institutions and the willingness of nations to pursue a shared understanding in the face of a divided world.

The United States' Changing Stance and Escalating Rhetoric

In the early days of the COVID-19 pandemic, the United States government's public stance on the virus's origin was one of caution. Initial official statements emphasized the virus's likely natural origins, in line with the views of many public health experts. However, as the pandemic continued to spread and political tensions with China intensified, the U.S. position began to shift. By mid-2020, a growing number of American officials started expressing concerns that COVID-19 may have originated from a lab in Wuhan. This shift marked the beginning of an intense period of escalating rhetoric and political maneuvering, significantly impacting public discourse on the virus's origins.

A critical turning point occurred in April 2020, when senior U.S. officials publicly suggested that COVID-19 might have been accidentally released from the Wuhan Institute of Virology. While initially based on limited intelligence, these statements quickly gained traction, fueled by rising anti-China sentiment and frustration over the economic and social toll of the pandemic. Then-Secretary of State Mike Pompeo was among the first high-profile officials to assert that there was "significant evidence" supporting the lab-leak theory, though he refrained from providing specific details, citing national security concerns. This statement marked a stark departure from the initial narrative of zoonotic transmission and injected a new sense of urgency into calls for a deeper investigation into the virus's origins.

As pressure mounted, U.S. intelligence agencies launched an inquiry into the possibility of a lab-based origin for COVID-19, tasked with exploring any evidence that might support or refute the lab-leak hypothesis. However, the initial findings, released later in 2020, were inconclusive. While the report acknowledged the lab-leak as a plausible scenario, it emphasized that there was insufficient evidence to definitively support or dismiss either the lab-leak theory or the natural origin theory. This inconclusiveness did little to quell speculation, instead fueling further debate both within the government and among the public.

The transition from one administration to another further intensified the spotlight on COVID-19's origins. While the Trump administration's stance had often included strong public accusations and demands for accountability from China, the Biden administration sought a more diplomatic approach. In May 2021, President Joe Biden ordered U.S. intelligence agencies to redouble their efforts in investigating the virus's origins, directing them to compile a report within 90 days. The decision reflected the administration's desire to resolve growing concerns around transparency and accountability, both domestically and internationally. President Biden emphasized the importance of finding the truth, not as a tool for blame but as a means to improve preparedness for future pandemics.

This renewed inquiry further polarized public opinion. In the U.S., political divisions influenced how people interpreted the lab-leak theory. Supporters of the theory argued that China's lack of transparency reinforced suspicions, while others believed the focus on the lab-leak theory risked stoking xenophobia and detracting from global cooperation on pandemic response. Media coverage of the theory fluctuated along partisan lines, with some outlets portraying the theory as highly plausible and even probable, while others cautioned against viewing it as the definitive explanation.

The global response to the U.S. intelligence investigation was mixed. Some allies expressed support for the effort, recognizing the importance of understanding COVID-19's origins. Other nations, particularly China, viewed the investigation with skepticism, arguing that it risked politicizing a scientific inquiry. Chinese officials criticized the U.S. investigation as a form of "virus origin tracing terrorism" and reiterated calls for the virus's origins to be explored in multiple countries, not just China. This rhetoric underscored the extent to which COVID-19's origins had become a diplomatic battleground, with each nation wary of implications that could tarnish their international reputation or influence future geopolitical alliances.

As the deadline for the intelligence report approached, public expectations for a definitive answer grew. However, the final report, released in August 2021, concluded with little more certainty than the earlier assessments. While some agencies leaned toward the lab-leak theory and others favored the natural origin hypothesis, no consensus emerged. The report underscored the need for additional data, particularly from China, and highlighted the challenges of investigating an event that had unfolded under conditions of high secrecy and limited access to information.

The inconclusive report left many questions unanswered, further fracturing public opinion on the matter. Some voices called for an international tribunal or independent investigation to pursue the issue further, while others argued that the focus should shift toward strengthening global health systems and preventing future outbreaks. Among scientists, calls for transparency remained strong, with many advocating for access to early data and samples that could clarify how the virus evolved and spread.

The U.S. government's evolving stance on COVID-19's origins illustrated the complex interplay of science, politics, and public perception in times of crisis. What had begun as a scientific inquiry into a pandemic's origins had morphed into a highly politicized debate, in which nations vied for control over the narrative, seeking to protect their interests and reputations. The lab-leak theory, once dismissed as improbable by many experts, had become a mainstream topic, shaping both international relations and the public's understanding of COVID-19. In many ways, the U.S. response reflected the broader challenges of navigating scientific uncertainty in a hyperpoliticized world, where the quest for truth often intersects with national priorities and global power dynamics.

The implications of this shifting stance extended beyond the immediate question of COVID-19's origins. It underscored the necessity for clear protocols in future pandemic investigations, emphasizing the importance of transparency, global cooperation, and a commitment to science free from political influence. The response also highlighted the enduring need for international organizations capable of coordinating unbiased inquiries, as well as the limitations faced when vital information is held back by national governments. Ultimately, the U.S. handling of the COVID-19 origin debate illustrated how critical it is for global health inquiries to be conducted with the utmost independence and openness, not just for accountability but to foster trust and prevent divisions that could hinder future pandemic responses.

In the end, the U.S. investigation, though inconclusive, underscored the importance of ongoing research, collaboration, and vigilance in preparing for pandemics. The experience served as a reminder that while science and politics may sometimes find themselves at odds, it is through unity and transparency that the world stands its best chance of facing such crises. As COVID-19 continued to spread, the origin question persisted, becoming a testament to both the challenges and the essential nature of cross-border, nonpartisan scientific inquiry in an interconnected world.

The Impact on International Trust and Future Pandemic Cooperation

As the COVID-19 pandemic unfolded, the question of its origins became an unexpected and contentious cornerstone in international relations. The debates over whether the virus emerged naturally or from a lab ignited profound suspicion and division among global powers, setting back years of scientific cooperation. This fracture went beyond mere diplomatic sparring; it marked a turning point in how nations viewed their collective responsibility to address future health crises. In a world where information-sharing could spell the difference between containment and catastrophe, the pandemic origins debate underscored both the necessity and the fragility of global trust.

Initially, global health cooperation seemed strong. Within the first months of the outbreak, organizations like the World Health Organization (WHO) coordinated efforts to study and contain the virus, working with countries on vaccine development, treatment guidelines, and public health strategies. However, as more information emerged about early outbreak management and the handling of data by various governments, tensions quickly escalated. Accusations surfaced that some countries, especially China, were not fully transparent, delaying critical information that could have helped contain the virus sooner. This perceived secrecy fanned skepticism worldwide, making it increasingly difficult for countries to align on strategies or rely on each other's data.

The growing mistrust over COVID-19's origins intensified calls for an independent, international investigation, prompting the WHO to undertake its own inquiry in early 2021. However, as researchers and officials faced obstacles in accessing key sites and data in China, the WHO's investigation became entangled in geopolitical concerns. Many Western countries, especially the United States, expressed frustration over what they saw as an opaque process. The Chinese government, for its part, countered with accusations of "politicizing the pandemic," suggesting that some nations were more interested in assigning blame than in genuinely finding the origin of the virus. This dynamic transformed the investigation into a political chess game, with each move influencing global perceptions about COVID-19's origins.

The consequences of this mistrust were profound, especially for scientific collaboration. For decades, scientists had relied on open access to data and resources across borders to tackle global health threats. But as COVID-19 spread, some nations tightened restrictions on sharing information and limited foreign researchers' access to their data, fearing that sensitive information could be used against them politically. This climate of suspicion hindered the development of a unified strategy for combating the virus. What had been a community of scientists driven by a common goal became fragmented, as individual nations prioritized self-protection over collaboration.

The disruption extended beyond the immediate response to COVID-19, casting a shadow over the future of international scientific partnerships. Collaborative efforts to monitor emerging diseases, for instance, faced new challenges as countries grew reluctant to fully engage in initiatives where data-sharing was key. Many experts warned that this retreat from cooperation could make it harder to detect and contain future outbreaks. Historically, the ability to share genetic sequencing information, viral samples, and epidemiological data had allowed scientists to recognize trends early and develop vaccines or treatments before diseases reached pandemic levels. Now, as nations became warier, the global community risked losing that proactive edge.

In response to these growing divisions, some global leaders began advocating for reforms aimed at restoring and safeguarding international trust in pandemic preparedness. Proposals included establishing new, neutral international bodies that could independently investigate disease outbreaks and develop standardized protocols for data-sharing. The idea was to create a system where nations could cooperate without feeling that their sovereignty or security was at risk. Additionally, some experts suggested an overhaul of the WHO's funding and governance structure to bolster its independence and strengthen its ability to conduct impartial investigations. While these reforms offered hope, implementing them posed a significant challenge. Nations had to weigh the immediate benefits of self-protection against the long-term advantages of collective action—a choice that became all the more difficult as political tensions lingered.

The pandemic's effect on international trust also had repercussions for public health messaging and vaccine distribution. Misinformation and conspiracy theories flourished as the public observed governments clashing over the virus's origins and handling. In many regions, public trust in health officials waned, exacerbating vaccine hesitancy and resistance to public health measures. Observers noted that if governments and global health organizations could not align on a unified narrative about COVID-19's origins and response, people were less likely to believe that measures like mask mandates or vaccination campaigns were in their best interest. As a result, some countries faced greater resistance to vaccination efforts, further complicating attempts to control the spread of the virus and prolonging the pandemic.

Perhaps one of the most lasting impacts of the COVID-19 origins debate will be on how the global community prepares for future pandemics. Experts have noted that the fragmented response to COVID-19 has underscored the importance of building a more resilient, cohesive framework for addressing health crises that cross borders. Some have suggested that instead of relying solely on governmental cooperation, future frameworks might benefit from involving a broader array of stakeholders, including academic institutions, private sector companies, and non-governmental organizations. By diversifying the entities involved in pandemic preparedness, the hope is to create a structure that is less vulnerable to the political fluctuations that so dramatically affected the response to COVID-19.

As the pandemic continued to unfold, it became increasingly clear that addressing global health threats requires a concerted effort not only to respond to crises but to build an infrastructure of trust and accountability that can withstand political turbulence. The COVID-19 origins debate has provided a stark reminder that without transparency, collaboration, and a commitment to science, the world risks being woefully unprepared for the next major health crisis. For many experts and policymakers, the pandemic has also underscored the need to rethink how we approach global health in a multipolar world, where the interests of individual nations are often at odds with the demands of collective well-being.

The question of COVID-19's origin remains unresolved, a potent symbol of both the strengths and weaknesses of the global health system. As countries continue to rebuild in the aftermath of the pandemic, the lessons learned about trust, transparency, and the delicate balance between scientific collaboration and national interest will shape how the world confronts future health challenges. In the end, the origins of COVID-19 may be less about pinpointing a definitive cause than about understanding what it reveals about our shared vulnerabilities—and how we might strengthen ourselves against them.

Chapter 8: Media Coverage and Public Perception

The Initial Media Response to COVID-19

In the early days of COVID-19, the world watched as a novel virus emerged in Wuhan, China, sparking intense media coverage. Initial reports trickled out with limited information about a mysterious illness causing pneumonia-like symptoms. These early media portrayals framed the virus as an unusual but localized outbreak, one of the many zoonotic viruses periodically emerging from animal markets in densely populated urban centers. Yet, as the situation unfolded, this local story rapidly escalated into a global event, with the media playing a crucial role in shaping public perception and understanding of COVID-19.

At first, local media within China, as well as some international outlets, hesitated to draw alarming conclusions. Reports from December 2019 and early January 2020 painted the virus as concerning but containable. Journalists relied on statements from Chinese health authorities who, in those initial days, downplayed the potential severity of the outbreak, focusing instead on control measures being taken. On January 9, 2020, the Chinese government publicly confirmed the emergence of a new coronavirus, a story that was picked up by global media but was not yet perceived as an urgent threat outside of Asia.

However, the tone shifted dramatically as cases began to rise and the virus showed signs of human-to-human transmission. When the World Health Organization (WHO) issued its first situation report on January 21, confirming human transmission in some cases, media outlets worldwide began to focus more on the virus's potential impact. In the following days, headlines began to reflect a growing sense of alarm, with more and more reports warning about a new "epidemic" and the need for proactive measures. By late January, international news agencies like CNN, BBC, and Reuters had started to report on the spread of the virus outside of China, covering cases in countries including Thailand, Japan, and the United States. This marked a significant turning point, with media coverage helping to fuel global awareness and concern.

As February progressed, reporting shifted from factual updates to deeper analysis and investigative journalism, seeking to answer the questions everyone had: Where had this virus come from? How deadly was it? How quickly could it spread? Media outlets sent reporters to Wuhan, and articles began to describe deserted streets, overwhelmed hospitals, and the lockdown of an entire city—a nearly unprecedented move that added to the gravity of the situation. News stories from that period often included interviews with healthcare workers and residents, painting a vivid picture of life in lockdown and the severe measures being implemented. This gave the public a glimpse into the crisis at ground zero and suggested that the virus posed a much larger threat than initially thought.

At the same time, however, the media faced challenges in balancing accurate reporting with responsible communication. Journalists and editors were aware of the need to inform the public without causing unnecessary panic. As a result, some outlets initially treaded carefully, framing the virus as a serious public health concern but not an existential threat. Yet as cases began to surge outside China, particularly in South Korea, Italy, and Iran, the tone of media reports became increasingly urgent, emphasizing the virus's rapid spread and the potential for a worldwide pandemic. This gradual escalation in reporting paralleled a rise in public awareness and anxiety, driven by the media's growing focus on the virus's spread and the potential for international outbreaks.

Interestingly, the media's role in shaping early perceptions of COVID-19 also highlighted disparities in how different regions and outlets approached the story. In countries with close economic ties to China, some media outlets adopted a more restrained tone, careful not to sensationalize the virus's origins. Other outlets, especially in Western countries, adopted a more cautionary approach, emphasizing the unknowns surrounding COVID-19 and the urgent need for preparedness. This divergence reflected not only different journalistic philosophies but also the varied political and economic interests that influenced media coverage.

By March 2020, as COVID-19 was officially declared a pandemic by the WHO, the media's role had shifted from merely reporting the news to actively informing and educating the public about preventive measures. Articles and news segments began to emphasize practices like social distancing, handwashing, and mask-wearing. This new focus represented a pivotal shift in public health messaging, with the media acting as a bridge between health authorities and the public. Across print, television, and online platforms, major news outlets dedicated significant resources to informing the public, often with daily updates on the virus's spread, new government guidelines, and recommendations from health experts.

The initial phase of COVID-19 media coverage thus illustrated the profound influence of the press in shaping public perception during a crisis. Journalists played an essential role in raising awareness, disseminating information, and providing a framework for understanding the pandemic's implications. Although initial reports were cautious and sometimes fragmented, the media's commitment to uncovering and reporting the truth allowed for a broader public understanding of COVID-19. This initial coverage laid the foundation for a more extensive and, at times, contentious exploration of the pandemic's origins, impact, and future implications, setting the stage for how the world would come to view one of the most significant health crises of the 21st century.

Evolution of Media Narratives on COVID-19 Origins

As the pandemic progressed, the question of COVID-19's origins became a focal point in global media coverage, evolving from tentative reports on a mysterious virus to a heated discourse over its potential sources. Initially, the dominant narrative focused on a natural origin theory, widely accepted among scientists and health organizations. However, as the months passed and more information emerged, this narrative began to shift, and media outlets across the world started to explore alternative theories, including the lab-leak hypothesis. This evolution in coverage was driven by scientific findings, political pressures, and an increasingly curious and skeptical public.

The earliest reports on COVID-19's origin almost universally echoed statements from Chinese officials and the World Health Organization (WHO), which pointed toward a zoonotic origin. The virus was thought to have jumped from animals to humans in a wet market in Wuhan, an explanation that aligned with previous outbreaks such as SARS, which also had animal origins. Media coverage during these initial months emphasized the scientific community's consensus on zoonosis and drew parallels to historical epidemics that had emerged through similar animal-to-human transmission. News articles illustrated these points with images of Wuhan's bustling Huanan Seafood Market, often accompanied by explanations of how close animal contact in such markets could create opportunities for viral mutation and transmission.

However, as the outbreak spread and more investigative reporting came to light, questions surrounding the Wuhan Institute of Virology (WIV) gained traction. Known for its work with bat coronaviruses, WIV became the subject of speculation, partly due to its proximity to the outbreak's initial epicenter. While the zoonotic origin theory remained widely accepted, certain media outlets, especially in Western countries, began probing the possibility of an accidental lab release. By April 2020, media narratives were becoming more complex and divided, as some journalists sought to investigate the lab's role, while others maintained that the natural origin theory was still the most plausible explanation.

This period saw a shift in journalistic tone, especially as government officials from countries like the United States began to publicly question the virus's origins and suggest the need for further investigation into the WIV. Statements from officials added fuel to the growing debate, prompting media outlets to explore both sides of the story. Publications began to feature experts who supported the natural origin theory alongside those open to the lab-leak hypothesis, introducing the public to a more nuanced view of the pandemic's potential origins. Investigative journalists faced obstacles as they tried to piece together the truth, particularly due to limited access to information within China and the politically charged nature of the topic. Nonetheless, stories began to emerge that detailed the types of research conducted at the WIV, including studies on bat coronaviruses that bore similarities to SARS-CoV-2, the virus responsible for COVID-19.

The evolution of media narratives was not only a result of scientific inquiry but also a reflection of political dynamics. Media outlets in countries that were critical of China's handling of the outbreak increasingly began to entertain the lab-leak theory, framing it as a plausible, if not likely, explanation for the pandemic's origins. In contrast, some outlets, especially within China or in regions with close economic ties to China, continued to emphasize the natural origin theory and questioned the motives behind the lab-leak discussions. This divergence in media perspectives highlighted how political affiliations could influence scientific narratives, with media reports often mirroring the stance of their home country's government.

As more attention turned to the lab-leak theory, public interest in uncovering COVID-19's origins grew. Social media played a significant role in amplifying both mainstream and fringe theories, creating an ecosystem where professional journalism and user-generated content intermingled. This led to further shifts in media coverage as journalists sought to address the swell of online speculation and conspiracy theories that accompanied the lab-leak discussion. In response, major news outlets began publishing articles that aimed to clarify the difference between scientifically grounded theories and unfounded conspiracy narratives, attempting to provide a balanced view amidst the noise. Articles explored the credibility of both the natural origin and lab-leak theories, often including input from virologists, epidemiologists, and experts in international relations to provide a well-rounded perspective.

By late 2020 and into 2021, the debate had escalated to the point where even scientific communities were divided, with new studies adding fuel to both sides. Media outlets began to report on investigations led by organizations like the WHO and independent research teams who were examining the virus's origins. Coverage of these investigations often portrayed a sense of anticipation, as each new study or finding was seen as a potential breakthrough in solving the mystery of COVID-19's origin. Journalists followed the progress of these investigations closely, publishing updates as soon as new information was released and occasionally speculating on the significance of particular findings.

As more time passed, the media's coverage of COVID-19's origins reflected a broader, ongoing quest for accountability and truth. Many outlets noted that identifying the origin was not merely an academic question but one with profound implications for global public health and future pandemic preparedness. By highlighting the complexities and uncertainties surrounding the virus's origin, journalists underscored the importance of transparency in scientific research and international collaboration.

In summary, the evolution of media narratives on COVID-19's origins illustrates how a straightforward story can transform into a multifaceted and contentious issue, shaped by scientific discovery, political tensions, and public curiosity. The media's role in navigating this complex narrative underscored both the power and responsibility of journalism in times of crisis, as journalists worked to inform, investigate, and ultimately, uncover the origins of one of the most significant events of the 21st century.

The Role of Social Media in Shaping Public Perception

Social media played an unprecedented role in shaping public perception of COVID-19's origins, giving voice to experts, skeptics, conspiracy theorists, and everyday citizens alike. With billions of users actively engaging on platforms like Twitter, Facebook, and Instagram, social media became both a battleground for debates and a breeding ground for speculation about the virus's origins. Unlike traditional media, which generally adhered to journalistic standards, social media allowed information to spread unchecked, creating a dynamic where facts and theories—whether substantiated or not—could rapidly gain momentum.

At the start of the pandemic, users turned to social media primarily for real-time updates on the virus's spread, sharing information on symptoms, prevention, and treatment. As the global population grappled with lockdowns, social media became a lifeline for communication, offering a sense of community amid isolation. However, the platform's very structure, designed to amplify viral content, soon facilitated the spread of theories regarding the virus's origins. Early discussions around COVID-19's genesis were largely dominated by the natural origin theory, mirroring the official stance of health organizations. Yet, as the pandemic progressed, the lab-leak hypothesis gained traction, spurred by the platform's algorithms that rewarded engaging, often sensational, content.

Among the first major social media discussions on the lab-leak theory emerged after comments made by political figures, some of whom speculated about possible connections between the virus and the Wuhan Institute of Virology (WIV). Tweets and posts from influential individuals spread rapidly, generating thousands of shares and igniting widespread discussion. For many users, the idea of a lab-leak was captivating, providing a potential answer to the mystery of COVID-19's sudden emergence. Hashtags like #WuhanLab and #LabLeakTheory trended intermittently as public interest spiked, encouraging further discussion and leading users to contribute their own theories, links, and personal analyses.

Social media's role in perpetuating the lab-leak theory was amplified by viral images and videos that purported to show "evidence" of the theory. One widely circulated video, for example, claimed to depict "hidden footage" from inside the WIV, although its authenticity was later debunked. Nonetheless, such posts added fuel to the fire, with some users interpreting the lack of clear answers as a sign of conspiracy or cover-up. This trend revealed an inherent flaw in social media: the platforms often prioritized engagement over accuracy, meaning misinformation could spread as easily—and sometimes more readily—than facts.

Platforms like Twitter allowed scientists and researchers to weigh in directly, offering both opportunities and challenges. On one hand, qualified virologists, epidemiologists, and public health experts had a direct channel to inform the public, correcting misunderstandings and clarifying data. On the other hand, some users selectively quoted scientists or misrepresented their statements to support pre-existing biases or agendas. As the debate grew more polarized, social media posts became an arena for ideological battles, where facts were often secondary to the desire to "win" the argument. This environment left many users feeling uncertain about whom to trust, contributing to a growing mistrust in both the scientific community and traditional media.

In response to the influx of COVID-19-related content, social media companies attempted to implement fact-checking measures. Platforms like Facebook and Twitter added warning labels to posts deemed misleading or false, a move intended to curb the spread of misinformation. However, these interventions had mixed results. While some users appreciated the effort to provide credible information, others saw the labels as censorship, sparking further controversy. As a result, conversations around COVID-19's origins grew more convoluted, with debates often focusing as much on the perceived suppression of information as on the actual content of the theories themselves.

The role of influencers and content creators also played a critical part in the public's perception of the virus's origins. YouTube and Instagram saw a surge in content from individuals claiming insider knowledge or conducting "independent investigations" into the lab-leak hypothesis. These videos, some reaching millions of views, often presented speculative or anecdotal evidence, yet they carried a degree of credibility among followers who trusted the creators. Personalities with large followings had the power to sway public opinion, often adding emotional or sensational elements that traditional news outlets avoided. For example, several well-known content creators made hour-long videos analyzing public reports, satellite images, and obscure documents, all in an effort to piece together a narrative that leaned toward the lab-leak theory. While some creators aimed for balanced analysis, others were quick to dismiss the natural origin theory, asserting that only a lab-leak explanation made sense.

One of the unintended consequences of this social media-fueled investigation was the reinforcement of echo chambers. Users who were inclined to believe one theory over the other tended to follow accounts and join groups that aligned with their beliefs, further solidifying their views. This phenomenon led to the formation of two camps: those who saw the lab-leak theory as a legitimate question needing investigation, and those who believed that such theories only served to distract from scientific consensus. Each group shared information that supported its stance, amplifying division and leaving little room for open, nuanced discussions.

By late 2020, social media had transformed the debate over COVID-19's origins from a scientific inquiry into a highly charged cultural and political issue. People were no longer simply asking "How did this pandemic begin?" Instead, the question had evolved to encompass issues of transparency, trust, and the role of government and scientific institutions in addressing global crises. For many users, social media became less a source of reliable information and more a lens through which to view the pandemic, colored by the prevailing sentiments of their chosen online communities.

In the end, social media's role in shaping public perception of COVID-19's origins underscored the double-edged nature of these platforms. On one hand, they democratized information, allowing a vast array of voices to participate in global conversations. On the other hand, they facilitated the rapid spread of unverified theories, amplifying misunderstandings and sowing doubt among the public. As society continues to grapple with the impact of COVID-19, the influence of social media on public discourse serves as a reminder of the profound responsibility that comes with wielding platforms capable of shaping perception on a global scale.

The Spread of Conspiracy Theories and Misinformation

As the COVID-19 pandemic progressed, a wave of conspiracy theories surrounding its origins began to emerge, taking on a life of their own. These theories filled a vacuum created by limited, evolving scientific information, a widespread sense of fear, and a global population increasingly connected—and sometimes misled—by the rapid spread of information online. What began as questions about the virus's origin soon escalated into an array of theories ranging from a lab-engineered pathogen designed for biowarfare to more far-fetched ideas involving coordinated global conspiracies. These theories propagated quickly, drawing on historical fears, geopolitical tensions, and the anxieties of a public facing an invisible, deadly threat.

Early in the pandemic, many people were eager to understand the virus's mysterious origins, but as science took time to offer explanations, frustration grew. Amid this void, theories purporting to "expose the truth" about the virus's genesis gained traction, appealing to a natural skepticism and a desire for straightforward answers. These theories found fertile ground in online spaces where fear, distrust, and curiosity collided. Social media platforms, forums, and even video-sharing sites became hubs for speculative content, where a simple claim could gather millions of views overnight. Videos alleging "undisclosed facts" or "government cover-ups" appeared in abundance, and with each share, like, or comment, the theories found new life, becoming embedded in the global narrative around COVID-19.

Some conspiracy theories claimed COVID-19 was the product of bioweapons research, supposedly designed either to weaken specific populations or to destabilize the global economy. This line of thought drew on historical instances of biological warfare and reflected an ingrained suspicion that governments or shadowy organizations might pursue such objectives under the guise of scientific research. Other theories suggested that pharmaceutical companies had engineered the virus in a plot to increase profits by later selling vaccines, feeding into existing concerns over corporate influence on public health. These narratives stoked a potent mix of fear and mistrust, encouraging people to view the crisis through the lens of hidden motives rather than as a purely biological or natural event.

Another popular theory revolved around the idea that COVID-19 was released deliberately to achieve specific global changes. Proponents of this view argued that lockdowns and pandemic-related restrictions were a trial run for broader social controls. Terms like "New World Order" began to appear in conversations, suggesting a coordinated attempt by powerful elites to manipulate society. For some, these theories offered a way to make sense of un-precedented restrictions and changes to daily life, framing them as part of a deliberate shift rather than a response to a crisis. Theories like these blended with long-standing conspiracy narratives, creating a complex web that linked COVID-19 with broader, pre-existing anxieties about government overreach and loss of individual free-doms.

The spread of these theories was accelerated by confirmation bias, the psychological tendency for individuals to seek out infor-mation that supports their pre-existing beliefs. As people searched for information online, algorithms designed to show users content aligned with their interests pushed similar videos, articles, and posts to the forefront of their feeds. This created echo chambers, where those predisposed to distrust institutions or believe in government conspiracies encountered more and more content reinforcing those views. While these digital spaces could provide community and vali-dation, they also intensified polarization, making it difficult for users to entertain alternative explanations. In the echo chambers of social media, even the wildest theories could appear increasingly plausible, as people found themselves surrounded by others who shared and reinforced their beliefs.

Mainstream media outlets struggled to combat the proliferation of misinformation and conspiracy theories. Fact-checking organiza-tions attempted to address the most prevalent myths, providing con-text and debunking falsehoods. However, these efforts sometimes backfired, as those committed to certain theories saw fact-check-ing as evidence of suppression or manipulation. For example, arti-cles disputing the lab-leak hypothesis early on were later viewed as censorship when the theory gained renewed attention from credible sources. For people already inclined to distrust mainstream narratives, this shift fueled further suspicion, as it seemed to confirm their belief that the truth was being hidden or controlled.

As conspiracy theories took root, public trust in scientific and health institutions faced erosion. While some saw organizations like the World Health Organization (WHO) as beacons of reliable information, others began questioning their motives. The shifting recommendations, changing mask mandates, and conflicting statements from various health agencies, though scientifically justified in many cases, fueled confusion and skepticism among those already inclined to question authority. This skepticism also affected public adherence to health guidelines, with some people refusing to follow recommendations they perceived as part of a broader, hidden agenda. In many ways, these conspiracy theories posed a parallel public health challenge: the more they spread, the more difficult it became for health authorities to enact policies and recommendations necessary to combat the virus itself.

Despite efforts to debunk them, conspiracy theories about COVID-19's origins persist, embedded in the minds of millions who view the virus as part of a larger, sinister plan. They illustrate the powerful role of narrative in times of uncertainty, as people seek out explanations that align with their values, fears, and worldviews. Social media has amplified these narratives, accelerating their spread in a way traditional media never could. The persistence of these theories raises questions about how societies can better address the spread of misinformation in future crises. As COVID-19 continues to impact lives worldwide, the rise of conspiracy theories surrounding its origins serves as a case study in the challenges of maintaining public trust amid a sea of conflicting information, highlighting the urgent need for transparency, effective communication, and trust-building in times of global crisis.

The Role of Social Media Companies and the Challenge of Moderation

As conspiracy theories and misinformation spread globally about COVID-19's origins, social media companies were thrust into an unprecedented role as gatekeepers of information. Unlike traditional news media, which had established editorial practices, social media companies were unprepared for the deluge of conflicting information, rapidly evolving science, and misinformation circulating on their platforms. This put companies like Facebook, Twitter, and YouTube in a difficult position: they needed to find a way to mitigate the spread of harmful misinformation without stifling open dialogue or overstepping boundaries around free expression.

Initially, social media companies approached COVID-19 misinformation with a laissez-faire attitude, erring on the side of open information flow. But as cases of COVID-19 skyrocketed worldwide and false information about cures, vaccines, and the virus's origins surged, these platforms faced mounting pressure from governments, health organizations, and the public to take a more active stance. When misinformation began to directly affect public health measures—such as false claims about the ineffectiveness of masks or the dangers of vaccines—social media companies had to balance between protecting public health and allowing free speech.

Facebook was one of the first to take significant action, instituting a "fact-checking" program to flag or remove posts containing dangerous falsehoods. This decision marked a turning point for the platform, and similar approaches were soon adopted by Twitter, YouTube, and others. Content flagged by reputable sources or fact-checkers appeared with warnings, or was taken down if deemed sufficiently dangerous. But these actions faced criticism from both sides: those wary of misinformation argued that more aggressive measures were needed, while others contended that such moderation violated free expression and promoted a bias against alternative viewpoints. Social media companies, caught in this complex landscape, faced criticism no matter what approach they took.

One significant challenge for social media companies was the evolving nature of COVID-19 information. Scientific understanding of the virus and its transmission was continually updated as researchers learned more. For instance, early statements from health authorities about masks or the virus's origins shifted over time, leading to understandable confusion. As scientific recommendations changed, so did the rules social media companies used to moderate content. However, this shifting landscape created a perfect storm for conspiracy theories: as guidelines changed, those who already doubted "official" narratives took it as confirmation that social media companies were censoring or manipulating information. Content moderation algorithms and policies were then criticized as fostering "information control," further fueling mistrust.

Moreover, content moderation algorithms themselves were imperfect, often mistakenly flagging credible information as false or allowing misinformation to slip through undetected. Social media companies began investing heavily in artificial intelligence to address these issues, but AI moderation tools had limitations. For instance, while AI can recognize certain keywords or patterns, it struggled with context—especially given the nuanced language of conspiracy theories. Posts suggesting that COVID-19 was part of a government agenda might be phrased in subtle ways, evading detection while still spreading doubt. Likewise, well-meaning posts questioning official statements were sometimes flagged as "misinformation," frustrating users who sought honest debate.

The role of fact-checkers added another layer to the moderation process, with organizations such as FactCheck.org and the International Fact-Checking Network partnering with social media companies to identify and label misinformation. However, fact-checking itself became contentious; certain users believed fact-checkers were biased, part of the perceived "mainstream" effort to silence dissent. To some, these warnings reinforced a belief that only one narrative was allowed, creating an "us versus them" mentality that deepened divisions. The presence of fact-checks on some posts and not others was enough for certain users to conclude that social media companies were complicit in controlling information.

Despite the backlash, social media companies continued to refine their moderation policies, creating "COVID-19 information centers" with verified resources from health organizations like the WHO and CDC. These centers directed users to reliable sources, aiming to provide clarity amid the storm of conflicting information. Platforms promoted these information centers in visible areas, hoping to reduce misinformation's reach by steering users to reputable sources. Yet, for some users, the very presence of these centers was viewed as an overt effort to control information—a further sign of perceived bias and censorship.

Social media companies faced another critical challenge: misinformation crossing international borders. In some countries, posts suggesting the virus was engineered by foreign governments to destabilize economies ignited tension, even leading to diplomatic disputes. To address misinformation on a global scale, social media companies had to navigate varying cultural, legal, and political landscapes, each with its own set of regulations and expectations. Misinformation in one country could have serious repercussions for international relations, requiring companies to implement tailored strategies for each region. This task added complexity, as what counted as misinformation in one country could be considered valid speculation in another.

In hindsight, the COVID-19 pandemic underscored the dual-edged sword of social media's power in the information age. The speed and reach of these platforms enabled valuable information to be shared widely, yet it also provided a fertile ground for conspiracy theories and misinformation. Social media companies found themselves at the epicenter of a global conversation about truth, information freedom, and the role of private companies in shaping public discourse. While they took strides to address the spread of harmful misinformation, their efforts also fueled debates around censorship, responsibility, and transparency that remain unresolved.

As society continues to grapple with questions about the origins of COVID-19 and the role of information in public health, the experience of the pandemic has highlighted a need for new frameworks in moderating content on social media. The balance between fostering open discussion and protecting public welfare remains a delicate one, and the COVID-19 pandemic may serve as a turning point for how information is managed in times of crisis. Social media companies, governments, and health organizations are left with the daunting task of finding a path forward that respects freedom of speech while safeguarding against the harmful impact of misinformation on global health and public trust.

Chapter 9: Scientific Investigations and Reports

Early Investigations by Global Health Authorities

In the early days of the COVID-19 pandemic, the world's leading health authorities found themselves in uncharted territory. The virus, which emerged in Wuhan, China, in late 2019, quickly spread to the farthest corners of the globe, sparking a race to understand its origins and prevent further outbreaks. The World Health Organization (WHO) and the Centers for Disease Control and Prevention (CDC) were among the first agencies to organize teams, protocols, and resources in an effort to address the new virus. In this unprecedented context, understanding where and how SARS-CoV-2, the virus causing COVID-19, originated became a matter of both public health and global security.

As the pandemic surged, the international community called upon the WHO to lead an investigation into the virus's origins. In response, the WHO assembled an international team of scientists and health experts, comprised of representatives from over a dozen countries, including the United States, Australia, and Japan. Their objective was not only to pinpoint the virus's source but to assess potential animal-to-human transmission paths, investigate the safety protocols of research institutions, and evaluate the role of Wuhan's wet markets, particularly the Huanan Seafood Wholesale Market, in the virus's spread. The WHO team faced significant challenges from the start, with China initially restricting the entry of external health experts into the country. Only after intense international pressure did China allow a WHO investigative team to visit in January 2021, over a year after the initial outbreak.

The team's mission, though heralded as a pivotal step in understanding COVID-19's origins, was limited in scope and hampered by logistical and political challenges. When WHO investigators arrived in Wuhan, they were presented with carefully curated data, and restrictions limited access to critical evidence, such as original patient samples and raw epidemiological data from the early days of the outbreak. The WHO team conducted field visits, interviewing local scientists and inspecting various sites, including the Huanan market, local hospitals, and research facilities like the Wuhan Institute of Virology. However, their access to these sites was guided, and their review of evidence was constrained by the circumstances, leaving the team with only a partial picture of the virus's emergence.

Despite these limitations, the team presented its preliminary findings in March 2021, laying out four potential origin pathways: direct zoonotic spillover (animal to human), transmission through an intermediate host species, introduction via the food supply chain, or a laboratory-associated incident. After their visit to Wuhan, the WHO team concluded that a natural zoonotic transmission was "likely to very likely" and ranked a lab-based origin as "extremely unlikely." However, the report admitted that due to data limitations, none of the proposed theories could be definitively proven or ruled out. This report garnered both praise and criticism: while it provided an organized framework to understand COVID-19's possible origins, many experts felt the report lacked conclusive answers, owing to the limited data and short duration of the investigation.

The WHO team's findings highlighted the limitations that scientists often face in politically charged environments. With China's restrictions on data access and an international demand for transparency, the WHO investigation was left to balance diplomacy and science. The global response to the report was mixed. Some governments accepted the findings as a reasonable first step, while others, including the U.S. and several European nations, voiced concerns about potential biases and gaps in the investigation. These concerns prompted a push for a more comprehensive, transparent, and independent inquiry into the origins of the virus, as many policymakers and scientists argued that full cooperation and unrestricted access to data were necessary to truly understand the virus's source.

Beyond political dynamics, the WHO report underscored the inherent difficulties in tracking the origins of a zoonotic virus. Scientists explained that identifying a definitive animal source can take years, if not decades. For instance, it took over a decade to trace the origin of SARS-CoV-1 to civet cats, and even longer to fully identify the animals linked to other zoonotic diseases. The lack of immediate access to raw epidemiological data, patient samples, and environmental evidence from Wuhan's wildlife markets meant that investigators had to rely on retrospective analyses, which, while insightful, could not substitute for real-time data. Furthermore, by the time the WHO team arrived in Wuhan, the Huanan Seafood Market had long been sanitized, erasing key pieces of physical evidence that could have clarified whether the virus had originated there.

Despite the difficulties and criticisms, the WHO's early investigation provided a framework for future inquiries, establishing key questions and areas for continued research. It also set the stage for further debates over the lab-leak theory versus zoonotic transmission, which would unfold in the months and years that followed. This report demonstrated the need for a global health approach that included transparency and unrestricted scientific collaboration—principles that would shape ongoing efforts to understand COVID-19's origins.

The limitations of the WHO's initial investigation also sparked discussions about preparedness for future pandemics. Leaders around the world recognized that efficient, transparent data sharing and early action are essential to effective pandemic response. The WHO's efforts emphasized that understanding the origins of COVID-19 was not only about solving a scientific mystery but also about learning from this experience to establish better protocols for future health crises.

Key Findings and Conclusions from International Research Teams

As the world grappled with the COVID-19 pandemic, independent international research teams quickly mobilized to investigate the origins of SARS-CoV-2, publishing their findings across scientific journals and news outlets. These groups, consisting of leading virologists, epidemiologists, and public health experts, aimed to provide objective, data-driven insights that could help the global community understand how this virus emerged and spread. Although their approaches and conclusions sometimes diverged, these teams collectively illuminated several critical aspects of the virus's origins and behavior. Their findings, while not definitive, contributed to a growing body of knowledge that would fuel the debate around the origins of COVID-19 for years to come.

One of the primary research pathways centered around genomic analysis. Researchers worldwide focused on sequencing the SARS-CoV-2 genome to identify potential clues about its evolutionary history. Early genomic studies revealed that SARS-CoV-2 shared approximately 96% of its genetic makeup with a known bat coronavirus, RaTG13, found in the Rhinolophus, or horseshoe bat, species. This genetic similarity strongly suggested that bats might be the original source of the virus, and scientists hypothesized that SARS-CoV-2 could have crossed to humans via an intermediary animal, as had been the case with other coronaviruses, such as SARS-CoV-1, which spread from bats to civet cats before reaching humans.

To investigate possible intermediary hosts, several research teams conducted studies at the animal markets in Wuhan, specifically the Huanan Seafood Market, which was linked to many of the early COVID-19 cases. Samples collected from the market revealed traces of SARS-CoV-2 on surfaces, suggesting the virus had indeed been present there. However, despite extensive testing of animal species, no direct animal source carrying the virus was identified. This lack of conclusive evidence of an intermediary species left scientists with an incomplete puzzle, fueling speculation that either the intermediary had not been sampled or that SARS-CoV-2 had found an alternative route to human transmission.

Other studies focused on examining SARS-CoV-2's unique characteristics that differentiate it from other coronaviruses. Researchers noted the virus's highly efficient human-to-human transmission, which they attributed partly to its spike protein—a critical component that allows the virus to bind to and enter human cells. Specifically, the virus's spike protein contains a furin cleavage site, a structural feature that increases its infectious potential. While similar structures have been observed in other viruses, the presence of the furin cleavage site in SARS-CoV-2 led some scientists to question whether it could have emerged purely through natural evolutionary processes. This structural anomaly became one of the focal points of the debate over whether SARS-CoV-2 could have been engineered or manipulated in a laboratory setting. However, numerous experts argued that natural evolutionary mechanisms could still account for the furin cleavage site, especially given the adaptability seen in coronaviruses.

As researchers analyzed these characteristics, another important line of inquiry emerged: the role of natural selection in the virus's rapid adaptation to humans. Some studies posited that SARS-CoV-2 might have circulated undetected in humans for months before being formally identified, during which time it adapted to human hosts. This hypothesis was supported by genetic evidence suggesting that the virus had undergone mutations that increased its affinity for human ACE2 receptors, the cellular entry points that SARS-CoV-2 targets in the body. If SARS-CoV-2 had indeed been silently circulating among humans, it could explain the virus's sudden appearance and swift spread, lending weight to the natural-origin theory over more speculative origins.

Amid these studies, a significant point of contention arose regarding whether SARS-CoV-2 could have been unintentionally released from a laboratory setting. In 2020, an international team led by respected virologist Dr. Kristian Andersen published a landmark study in *Nature Medicine* stating that, based on available genomic data, SARS-CoV-2 was "not a laboratory construct or a purposefully manipulated virus." The study argued that SARS-CoV-2's genetic features, including the spike protein's furin cleavage site, bore hallmarks of natural evolution rather than engineering. This paper temporarily bolstered the argument against a lab origin, suggesting that while questions remained, the evidence leaned toward a natural zoonotic origin. Nevertheless, the report did not close the door on the possibility of an accidental lab release involving a naturally occurring virus, which would continue to fuel ongoing investigations.

As research continued, these scientific findings highlighted both the advances and limitations of virus origin studies. The use of advanced genomic sequencing enabled scientists to trace the evolutionary history of SARS-CoV-2 with unprecedented precision, but the search for a definitive origin was hampered by factors beyond the scientific community's control. Limitations in data, such as the inability to access certain samples from China, the destruction of early patient samples, and the lack of direct evidence linking the virus to a specific animal intermediary, hindered conclusive results. Without access to these critical data points, scientists could only form educated hypotheses, leaving some questions unanswered.

Despite the challenges, the collective efforts of these international research teams underscored the importance of transparency and collaboration in pandemic response. Their findings, while sometimes inconclusive or controversial, advanced our understanding of zoonotic viruses and emphasized the need for robust monitoring and regulation of animal markets, wildlife trade, and laboratory safety protocols. As scientists and policymakers alike grappled with the pandemic's aftermath, the work of these research teams would serve as a reminder of the complexity of tracing viral origins—and the vital role that science plays in guiding public health policy.

The findings from these early investigations laid the groundwork for further studies, debates, and policy decisions. While scientists were unable to pinpoint the exact origin of SARS-CoV-2, their work illuminated the pathways through which viruses emerge and adapt to human hosts. These efforts also highlighted the critical need for preparedness and collaboration in confronting future outbreaks, setting the stage for ongoing research and international discussions around pandemic prevention and response.

Independent Reviews and Multinational Collaboration

As the COVID-19 pandemic intensified, the international community recognized the urgent need for a coordinated, independent review of the virus's origins. With health systems overwhelmed and economies staggering under lockdown measures, the stakes for understanding the virus's emergence were higher than ever. Amid calls for transparency, independent review organizations, multinational task forces, and scientific coalitions joined forces, initiating efforts to assess available data and propose pathways to clarity on SARS-CoV-2's origins.

In early 2021, the World Health Organization (WHO), the primary international health authority, dispatched a team of scientists and experts to Wuhan, China—the first known epicenter of the outbreak—to conduct a joint study with Chinese health officials. This delegation consisted of 17 international specialists in fields ranging from epidemiology and animal health to virology and biosecurity, each selected to bring both scientific rigor and independence to the inquiry. The mission aimed to uncover the earliest signs of SARS-CoV-2, determine potential animal sources, and evaluate the theory of lab involvement.

Upon arriving in Wuhan, the team encountered logistical and diplomatic challenges that underscored the complexities of international collaboration in a politically sensitive investigation. Access to data was restricted, and key records or biological samples were either unavailable or incomplete. Many global observers noted that China's reluctance to share certain data fueled suspicions of obfuscation. Despite these challenges, the WHO delegation focused on several critical avenues of inquiry: examining early COVID-19 cases, assessing the Huanan Seafood Market's role, investigating regional animal farms as potential sources, and visiting the Wuhan Institute of Virology (WIV).

The final report, released in March 2021, provided a nuanced view that outlined multiple hypotheses while also emphasizing limitations due to incomplete data. The study suggested four potential pathways for the virus's emergence: a direct zoonotic spillover from animals to humans, an intermediary animal host, introduction through the cold food chain, and the possibility of a laboratory incident. Although the lab-leak theory was deemed "extremely unlikely," the report classified zoonotic origins as "likely to very likely," given the virus's genetic similarity to known bat coronaviruses. However, the findings faced criticism, with some scientists and government officials questioning the report's methodology, noting that without full transparency, any conclusion remained tentative.

In response to these critiques, several independent reviews and scientific organizations continued pursuing additional lines of investigation, pushing for increased data access. In the United States, the National Institutes of Health (NIH), Centers for Disease Control and Prevention (CDC), and Office of the Director of National Intelligence (ODNI) launched internal studies to examine SARS-CoV-2's origins, reviewing intelligence reports and coordinating with global researchers. These organizations sought to clarify the virus's beginnings through a combination of genomic analysis, epidemiological mapping, and expert consultations.

Moreover, in June 2021, U.S. President Joe Biden ordered a 90-day intelligence review to address persisting questions about the origins of COVID-19, including the lab-leak hypothesis. This review, led by a coalition of intelligence agencies, aimed to analyze all available data, considering both scientific evidence and intelligence reports. The final report from this task force did not arrive at a definitive conclusion but highlighted two predominant theories—the zoonotic origin and the lab-leak hypothesis—while calling for further investigation. The report stressed the need for greater cooperation from China, emphasizing that without complete transparency, understanding the exact origin of SARS-CoV-2 might remain out of reach.

While governmental reviews sought answers, multinational coalitions of scientists continued to study the virus independently. A group of 18 prominent scientists published a letter in *Science* journal in May 2021, calling for a more thorough investigation into both natural and lab-based origins. This letter underscored the importance of exploring all possibilities and argued that no single hypothesis should be prematurely dismissed. Their position was clear: as long as uncertainties remained, so did the need for open, unbiased scientific inquiry. This coalition advocated for collaborative efforts that transcended political agendas, underscoring the importance of a science-driven approach.

The absence of definitive answers in early investigations spurred other global bodies to contribute to the discussion. The Lancet COVID-19 Commission—a special task force created to assess the pandemic's trajectory, response, and impact—assembled a working group of virologists, epidemiologists, and public health experts to examine the origins of SARS-CoV-2. However, even this task force experienced internal tensions, with debates emerging about the impartiality of some members and the influence of external factors. Ultimately, these challenges highlighted the need for a transparent and impartial approach, one free from political bias, if such investigations were to provide credible answers.

The collective efforts of these groups underscored the reality that investigating a pandemic's origin is a complex and often contentious process, especially amid geopolitical tensions. Scientists and policy-makers alike acknowledged that without full data access and transparency, determining the true origins of SARS-CoV-2 would remain challenging. However, the sustained efforts by independent and multinational bodies demonstrated the power of global collaboration. Despite obstacles, these reviews and coalitions provided valuable insights, contributing to a broader understanding of zoonotic spillover, lab safety standards, and the global scientific response to novel pathogens.

The investigations also left a lasting impact on international discourse regarding future pandemic preparedness. Calls for increased transparency, especially in research and data sharing across borders, grew louder. Governments and scientific communities worldwide recognized the urgency of building stronger global health frameworks and establishing protocols for swift data sharing in the event of future outbreaks.

In the absence of conclusive answers, the collaborative work of independent reviews and multinational bodies reaffirmed a critical lesson: understanding a pandemic's origin is not solely a scientific endeavor but a global commitment requiring diplomacy, transparency, and resilience. The question of SARS-CoV-2's beginnings might not yet be fully resolved, but the groundwork laid by these collaborative investigations continued to drive forward the quest for answers, illustrating the essential nature of international cooperation in safeguarding public health.

The Role of Transparency and Data Access

As COVID-19 swept across continents, the world quickly realized that scientific transparency and unhindered data access were crucial not only to addressing the pandemic's immediate effects but also to understanding its origin. Yet, in the quest to uncover how SARS-CoV-2 first made its way into humans, researchers and investigators repeatedly encountered roadblocks. These barriers were not merely incidental; they were symptomatic of broader geopolitical tensions and fears over national reputations, contributing to a fragmented approach to understanding the virus's origins.

At the heart of the debate was the role of China, which was simultaneously the initial epicenter of the virus and a major player in international research. The lack of immediate transparency surrounding COVID-19's earliest cases, potential intermediary hosts, and laboratory research from Chinese authorities fueled suspicion. This opacity gave rise to a diverse array of theories—from zoonotic spillovers involving animal hosts to more controversial theories, including the lab-leak hypothesis. Many scientists, public health officials, and governments argued that unrestricted access to early data, patient samples, and laboratory records would be essential in determining the virus's origin with greater certainty.

One of the primary challenges was gaining access to original records from the Huanan Seafood Wholesale Market in Wuhan, where several of the first known cases were traced. While initial investigations sought to collect samples and analyze the presence of SARS-CoV-2 within the market environment, access was limited. Despite its significance, information about animal vendors, supply chains, and environmental samples was not fully available to international investigators. This lack of transparency contributed to ongoing questions about whether the market itself was the original source of transmission or simply a highly trafficked location where a preexisting virus spread among humans.

Data access challenges extended beyond the market. Investigators sought records from the Wuhan Institute of Virology (WIV), given the facility's role in researching coronaviruses closely related to

SARS-CoV-2. In particular, research led by Dr. Shi Zhengli, a prominent virologist at WIV, had previously identified and isolated bat coronaviruses with genetic similarities to SARS-CoV-2. However, requests for data on the institute's virus repository, as well as its operational safety protocols, met with resistance. Officials cited national security concerns, and WIV representatives reiterated their adherence to stringent biosafety protocols. Nonetheless, in the absence of full access, skepticism persisted among those advocating for a thorough exploration of the lab-leak theory.

International organizations, particularly the World Health Organization (WHO), found themselves in a precarious position as they attempted to balance diplomacy with demands for transparency. While the WHO's 2021 visit to Wuhan was a step forward, the delegation encountered restrictions that limited its access to raw data. The team's final report acknowledged these limitations, leading to criticism from scientists and policymakers worldwide who argued that without full transparency, any conclusions drawn were incomplete at best. Calls for greater openness became louder, with the international community stressing that transparency was not merely an act of good faith—it was essential to building trust and preventing future pandemics.

Despite these barriers, some countries and organizations responded with initiatives aimed at bolstering transparency and collaborative research. In the United States, for example, the National Institutes of Health (NIH) and the Centers for Disease Control and Prevention (CDC) intensified their genomic research on SARS-CoV-2, with an emphasis on sequencing efforts to track mutations and understand viral evolution. Meanwhile, collaborations between scientists across various countries led to public data repositories that contained thousands of viral genome sequences, enabling independent researchers to study viral mutations and make inferences about the virus's potential origins.

The push for data transparency also underscored a growing discourse about the ethics of scientific research in an interconnected world. Many in the global scientific community argued that data related to pathogens with pandemic potential should not be restricted by national borders or political interests. Calls emerged for a standardized, international protocol for data-sharing in response to outbreaks, emphasizing that withholding information during a global health crisis was both ethically questionable and counterproductive.

One proposal gaining traction was the establishment of an independent, global task force under the United Nations or a similar body, tasked explicitly with investigating future outbreaks with full data access across borders. This task force would be empowered to work independently of political influence, armed with the authority to request and obtain critical data directly from affected regions. Such a framework, supporters argued, could mitigate the delays, suspicions, and controversies that plagued the COVID-19 origins investigation. However, the concept faced pushback from countries wary of international oversight and concerns over sovereignty, highlighting the complexities of implementing truly open scientific practices in a divided world.

Despite these tensions, the collective global response signaled a shift toward greater accountability. While transparency remained a contentious issue, the experiences of the COVID-19 pandemic underscored that no country is immune to the impacts of a global health crisis, and thus, cooperation and openness are indispensable. This realization spurred advocacy for policies that prioritize pandemic preparedness and data-sharing. Legislative measures, proposals for international agreements, and funding for pathogen research all began to reflect a greater awareness of the need for transparent scientific investigation in the face of emerging infectious diseases.

In retrospect, the obstacles to data access and transparency highlighted during the COVID-19 origins investigation may well serve as lessons for future outbreaks. The pandemic exposed not only the limitations of current systems but also the critical importance of an open, collaborative approach to scientific inquiry. Achieving transparency in pandemic origins investigations may be fraught with challenges, yet it remains a key component of global health security.

The legacy of COVID-19, in terms of data access and transparency, has ignited a movement among scientists, health organizations, and policymakers to address these gaps. As the world prepares for future outbreaks, the hope is that these hard-earned lessons will drive progress toward a new era in which open data, unimpeded investigation, and global cooperation become the norm, not the exception.

Ongoing Research and Future Directions

As the world grapples with the lasting impacts of COVID-19, understanding the virus's origins has become a focal point of scientific inquiry, political debate, and ethical reflection. While immediate pandemic control took precedence in 2020 and 2021, researchers and organizations worldwide have since poured resources into tracing SARS-CoV-2's origins with unprecedented rigor. This section explores the ongoing research into COVID-19's roots, the new methodologies applied in viral origin studies, and the future directions that could reshape how we respond to—and possibly prevent—similar pandemics.

One of the most promising directions in SARS-CoV-2 origin research lies in genetic and molecular analysis. Modern genetic sequencing allows scientists to map the virus's mutations and compare its genetic structure to thousands of related viruses stored in databases globally. This approach enables researchers to trace potential evolutionary paths and locate connections to viruses found in animal reservoirs, particularly bats and other mammals with similar viral strains. A comprehensive comparative analysis of SARS-CoV-2 with other coronaviruses found in nature could provide insights into whether the virus's adaptation to human hosts occurred naturally or involved laboratory influence.

Alongside genetic mapping, environmental sampling has become a key focus area. Environmental samples from sites like the Huanan Seafood Market, areas with dense bat populations, and even wastewater sources continue to undergo analysis for viral remnants. By examining viral RNA fragments present in these environments, scientists can better understand SARS-CoV-2's behavior and movement prior to and during the outbreak in humans. Moreover, ongoing studies in places known to have high bat populations in Southeast Asia and other regions aim to uncover similar coronaviruses that could further shed light on the virus's ancestry. This research holds potential to uncover "viral hot zones," places where future zoonotic transmissions are most likely to occur.

In tandem with this, advances in serological testing—testing blood for antibodies—may allow researchers to retrospectively analyze samples from people who were ill with respiratory symptoms prior to the initial outbreak. This could help detect early cases that might not have been identified at the time as COVID-19, shedding light on how and when the virus first entered the human population. These tests are also critical for pinpointing the timeframe and potential patient zero in cases where known transmissions were recorded in multiple locations early on. Such studies could illuminate whether isolated cases of COVID-19 occurred outside Wuhan in the months leading up to the official recognition of the outbreak.

Technological advancements in artificial intelligence (AI) and machine learning are also reshaping viral origin research. By analyzing massive datasets from diverse sources, AI can help scientists detect patterns, similarities, and anomalies across viral sequences and epidemiological data. For instance, AI models can identify correlations in zoonotic spillover events by evaluating environmental factors, human population density, and wildlife movement patterns. In theory, these models could predict regions or species at risk for future zoonotic transmission, aiding in preemptive monitoring and preventive measures.

The expansion of collaborative networks among scientists has become another cornerstone of pandemic origin research. COVID-19 catalyzed an unprecedented level of international cooperation among laboratories, universities, and health organizations. Initiatives like the Global Virome Project aim to document and sequence viruses in wildlife across the globe, creating an extensive repository that researchers can access to analyze potential future threats. These collaborations seek not only to find SARS-CoV-2's origin but also to prepare humanity for the next pandemic by cataloging known pathogens and conducting proactive viral surveillance in wildlife.

However, future research in this field is not without ethical concerns and challenges. Investigating the origins of highly pathogenic viruses often requires working with live viruses in high-containment labs, which raises biosafety risks. Some scientists and bioethicists argue for stricter regulations on "gain-of-function" research, which involves modifying pathogens to study their transmissibility or virulence. While this research can provide invaluable insights, it also raises questions about the balance between scientific curiosity and potential risks to public health. As the international community navigates these debates, consensus on safer research protocols and stricter oversight could help reduce risks associated with studying potentially pandemic-causing agents.

Global health policy is another area primed for transformation as a result of COVID-19 origin studies. Health organizations and governments are increasingly acknowledging the importance of transparency and accountability in infectious disease research. Proposals for new guidelines on data-sharing and global investigations have gained traction, calling for legally binding agreements that ensure countries make critical data available in the event of an outbreak. If implemented, such policies could help overcome some of the obstacles that hampered early investigations into COVID-19's origins, ensuring that scientific inquiry can proceed unimpeded by political or national interests.

In addition to these procedural shifts, there's a growing call for broader education about zoonotic diseases and pandemic preparedness at both the public and professional levels. Organizations like the World Health Organization (WHO) and Centers for Disease Control and Prevention (CDC) are spearheading initiatives to better equip healthcare professionals, government officials, and the general public to respond swiftly to future outbreaks. This effort aims to instill a proactive mindset that could reduce response times, encourage compliance with safety protocols, and ultimately prevent the global upheaval seen with COVID-19.

While definitive answers to COVID-19's origins may take years, if not decades, the ongoing research efforts underscore the pandemic's transformative impact on global health science. The scientific community now faces a unique opportunity: to forge new partnerships, adopt cutting-edge research techniques, and establish global protocols that could dramatically improve pandemic response. Although the mystery surrounding SARS-CoV-2's origin remains unresolved, the collective determination to prevent another crisis of this magnitude signals a new era of commitment to global health security.

The pursuit of knowledge about COVID-19's beginnings is far from a purely academic exercise; it's a pivotal chapter in humankind's resilience against future threats. By investing in this research, enhancing global collaborations, and setting rigorous standards for transparency and safety, the world may ultimately succeed not only in answering the questions surrounding COVID-19 but also in building a legacy of preparedness for generations to come.

Chapter 10: Ethical and Moral Considerations

The Ethics of High-Risk Research

As the world has come to grips with the scale of the COVID-19 pandemic, a new set of questions has emerged around the ethics of high-risk virology research. In particular, "gain-of-function" research, which involves manipulating pathogens to increase their transmissibility or virulence to better understand potential pandemic threats, has taken center stage in public and scientific debate. Proponents argue that such research is essential for staying ahead of natural viral evolution by identifying vulnerabilities in pathogens and developing corresponding vaccines and treatments. However, critics contend that the risks of accidental or even deliberate release are too great and that scientific curiosity should not outweigh the moral imperative to avoid harm to society.

Gain-of-function research, which deliberately enhances a virus's capabilities, is inherently controversial because of the high-stakes consequences it entails. On one hand, the rationale for conducting such research is compelling: by understanding how viruses might evolve in nature, scientists can better prepare to combat them. For example, studying mutations that might make a virus more contagious can inform public health measures and accelerate vaccine development. In this way, gain-of-function research can be seen as a proactive defense mechanism, arming humanity with knowledge that might someday prevent a pandemic.

On the other hand, critics question whether the benefits of this type of research justify its profound risks. Gain-of-function experiments typically require high-containment laboratories, such as Biosafety Level 3 or 4 labs, equipped with stringent protocols to ensure safety. However, even these precautions do not eliminate the risk of accidental release, as past incidents have demonstrated. In 2014, for example, vials of smallpox were found at a U.S. Food and Drug Administration lab, raising concerns about the management of dangerous pathogens even within advanced, regulated facilities. Additionally, there is the sobering possibility of intentional misuse of gain-of-function research findings, which could potentially be weaponized. Opponents argue that even the possibility of such catastrophic outcomes renders gain-of-function research ethically indefensible.

The ethical debate over gain-of-function research is rooted in the classic philosophical problem of balancing the potential good of scientific advancement with the imperative to avoid harm. Utilitarian ethics, which emphasize maximizing the greater good, might support gain-of-function research on the basis that the knowledge it yields could prevent future pandemics, saving millions of lives. However, a deontological perspective, which holds that certain actions are inherently right or wrong regardless of outcomes, might contend that creating or enhancing a potentially deadly pathogen is morally unacceptable, irrespective of the intended benefits.

A series of case studies from other areas of high-risk scientific research can provide additional context to this debate. Nuclear energy research, for instance, has long grappled with ethical questions similar to those facing gain-of-function research in virology. While nuclear energy offers a powerful solution to the global energy crisis, the potential for devastating accidents, such as those at Chernobyl and Fukushima, looms large. Like virology, nuclear energy has benefitted from rigorous international oversight, safety protocols, and ethical guidelines aimed at minimizing risk. Nevertheless, these cases serve as a reminder that even the most controlled environments carry inherent dangers, prompting reflection on the acceptability of certain scientific pursuits.

Ultimately, the ethical debate over high-risk research, including gain-of-function studies, hinges on the issue of trust in scientific institutions and regulatory frameworks. How confident can society be that research facilities and governments are upholding rigorous safety standards? What degree of transparency should accompany such high-risk work, and who bears the responsibility if an accident or misuse occurs? As the COVID-19 pandemic has shown, the consequences of viral outbreaks extend far beyond health, touching every aspect of social and economic life. Consequently, gain-of-function research, while potentially valuable, requires an unprecedented level of ethical scrutiny, public oversight, and precaution.

Section 1 underscores the complexity and urgency of these ethical considerations. As scientific knowledge continues to expand, so too does the need for a moral framework capable of guiding research in a way that prioritizes both progress and public safety.

Transparency and Public Accountability in Research

In an era where science and public policy are intertwined, transparency has become essential for maintaining trust in high-stakes research. This is particularly true in pandemic-related research, where the global implications are profound, and the public has a vested interest in understanding the nature and purpose of the research being conducted. Yet, despite the recognized need for transparency, significant challenges persist, ranging from concerns about national security to the competitive nature of scientific discovery. In exploring these challenges, it becomes clear that a lack of transparency not only risks public trust but also increases the potential for misinformation, ultimately hindering both scientific progress and societal preparedness.

Transparency in scientific research is based on the principle that the public has a right to know what is being studied, especially when such research can impact health and safety on a global scale. For instance, had there been greater openness about the specific studies being conducted on coronaviruses before COVID-19 emerged, it is possible that early public health measures could have been informed by more specific data, potentially mitigating some of the pandemic's initial spread. This example underscores the need for transparency not as a mere ethical preference but as a practical necessity in today's interconnected world, where rapid access to information is critical in managing public health threats.

However, several barriers make complete transparency difficult to achieve. One of the most significant is the concern over national security. In cases where research involves potentially dangerous pathogens, scientists and governments may withhold details to prevent the data from falling into the wrong hands. While this rationale is understandable, it raises ethical questions. For instance, does the potential for bioterrorism justify withholding information from the public? And how much secrecy is warranted before it begins to infringe on the public's right to be informed? As pandemics can spread without regard to borders, these questions point to a need for balance: researchers must protect sensitive data but also strive for openness whenever feasible.

Another factor that complicates transparency is the competitive nature of scientific discovery. For many researchers and institutions, there is pressure to secure funding, publish groundbreaking findings, and gain recognition. This competitive environment can lead to a culture of secrecy, where the sharing of data and findings becomes secondary to the pursuit of accolades and funding. For instance, if scientists discover mutations in a virus that make it more transmissible to humans, they may feel pressured to keep the findings confidential until they can publish, potentially delaying crucial information that could be vital to public health agencies. Here, the ethical dilemma becomes one of prioritizing scientific recognition against immediate public benefit.

The lack of transparency can also fuel conspiracy theories and public distrust. During the COVID-19 pandemic, the opaque nature of some early communications, especially regarding the virus's origins, fueled speculation and allowed misinformation to spread. With little clear information available, the public began to fill in gaps with conjecture, leading to rumors and false narratives that complicated public health efforts. This points to an essential truth in public health communication: when information is withheld, people tend to seek answers independently, often turning to unreliable sources that can further distort the public understanding of scientific realities.

One example of the ethical necessity of transparency can be seen in the field of environmental research, where public data has helped communities and policymakers make informed decisions. For instance, data on pollution levels, available through environmental health studies, has empowered local communities to advocate for policy changes. This model of open research not only enables informed public participation but also strengthens the relationship between scientists and society. Adapting this approach to pandemic-related research could foster a similar sense of shared purpose, where the public becomes an informed partner in addressing global health challenges.

In conclusion, transparency and public accountability are more than ethical ideals; they are crucial components of an effective and trusted scientific process. To navigate the challenges of transparency in pandemic-related research, scientific institutions must strive for a balanced approach that protects sensitive information while providing the public with clear, accurate, and timely information. By fostering a culture of openness, researchers can help mitigate distrust, combat misinformation, and ensure that the benefits of high-stakes research extend as broadly and equitably as possible.

The Role of Regulatory Oversight and International Collaboration

As scientific research pushes further into the realms of genetic engineering and virology, regulatory oversight has become a central focus for both national governments and international agencies. The goal of regulatory frameworks is to ensure that high-risk research, particularly studies involving infectious pathogens, is conducted under strict safety and ethical standards. The COVID-19 pandemic highlighted both the necessity and the complexity of regulating such research. In an increasingly interconnected world, regulatory oversight alone cannot guarantee safety; international collaboration is essential. Yet, establishing uniform standards across countries, each with its own scientific priorities and political agendas, remains a formidable challenge.

Effective regulatory oversight involves not only strict protocols within research facilities but also a thorough system of checks and accountability. Within high-containment laboratories, stringent biosafety protocols and equipment are used to prevent accidental re-leases of dangerous pathogens. Researchers working in these labs fol-low multiple layers of safety measures, from the use of protective equipment to specialized containment facilities like Biosafety Level 3 (BSL-3) and Biosafety Level 4 (BSL-4) labs, which are designed to handle the most infectious agents. Oversight bodies, including na-tional health agencies and ethics committees, are tasked with reg-ularly evaluating the safety practices of these labs. However, the effectiveness of these regulatory frameworks depends on rigorous, transparent enforcement—a point that was underscored by previous incidents where safety lapses led to public health risks.

Despite national-level regulations, the global nature of pan-demics has revealed the need for international standards. Pathogens do not respect borders, and an outbreak originating in one country can quickly spread worldwide, as COVID-19 demonstrated. Inter-national collaboration is therefore critical in establishing uniform re-search protocols and biosafety standards that are upheld globally. Organizations such as the World Health Organization (WHO) and the World Organisation for Animal Health (OIE) work to promote international standards for laboratory safety and pathogen handling, providing a shared foundation for countries to follow. However, while these organizations can issue guidelines, enforcement is largely left to individual nations, creating discrepancies in how research is conducted and regulated globally.

One prominent example of the challenges in international over-sight is the difficulty of conducting investigations across borders. The origins of COVID-19 brought this issue into sharp relief, as sci-entists from multiple countries were eager to investigate the initial outbreak in Wuhan. Yet geopolitical tensions and varying national policies complicated these efforts. Transparency and cooperation be-tween nations proved to be critical hurdles. Some nations were hesitant to grant international investigators full access to laboratories and data, leading to suspicions and accusations that have clouded the investigation's findings. Without transparent collaboration, achieving a unified approach to biosecurity and research ethics remains an elusive goal.

Beyond regulatory policies, there is an urgent need for ethical agreements on what constitutes acceptable research in virology and genetics. Gain-of-function research, which involves altering a pathogen to study its potential effects on humans, illustrates the ethical quandary faced by the global scientific community. The U.S. and several other countries have implemented moratoriums and funding restrictions on certain types of gain-of-function research, but policies vary widely. In some countries, research that is highly regulated or prohibited in others may proceed with fewer restrictions. This regulatory inconsistency not only poses ethical dilemmas but also presents a significant risk to global biosecurity, as research conducted under less stringent oversight could still result in worldwide consequences if safety breaches occur.

International collaboration is further complicated by the competitive nature of scientific research. Countries often wish to maintain scientific dominance and may withhold information or limit access to their facilities. In areas of high-stakes research, such as virology, there is sometimes reluctance to share findings openly, out of fear that other nations may misuse or exploit sensitive data. These challenges underscore the need for a standardized and cooperative global approach to high-risk research. Initiatives like the Global Health Security Agenda (GHSA) have made strides in promoting global health security through collaboration, but more work is needed to ensure that international partnerships are robust enough to withstand both scientific and political pressures.

In summary, regulatory oversight and international collaboration are vital components of a responsible approach to high-risk research in virology and genetics. While national-level regulatory frameworks provide essential safeguards, the need for consistent, enforced international standards is increasingly clear. Only through cooperation, transparency, and shared ethical guidelines can the global community hope to manage the risks associated with cutting-edge biological research and prevent future outbreaks. The COVID-19 pandemic serves as a stark reminder that, in matters of public health, we are only as safe as our weakest link. International collaboration, reinforced by stringent regulatory oversight, remains the most viable path toward a safer, more resilient global health landscape.

Balancing Innovation and Risk in High-Stakes Research

In scientific exploration, balancing innovation and risk is a continual challenge, particularly when it comes to research involving pathogens. The rapid advancements in fields like virology, genomics, and biotechnology have opened doors to unprecedented insights and capabilities, enabling scientists to study viruses and pathogens with precision that was unimaginable just a few decades ago. This research holds immense potential for good, from developing vaccines to understanding disease transmission. However, it also carries inherent risks, especially in high-stakes research where unintended consequences could lead to global health emergencies.

The benefits of innovative research in virology are clear. Studying pathogens in controlled environments allows researchers to observe how viruses might evolve, jump between species, or increase their transmissibility. These studies can lead to breakthroughs that strengthen humanity's defenses against pandemics. For example, by studying the genetic mutations that enable viruses to cross species, scientists can develop predictive models to identify which pathogens might pose the greatest threats. Such models are invaluable to public health agencies worldwide, allowing them to prioritize resources, prepare targeted responses, and initiate surveillance measures that could avert widespread outbreaks.

Yet, the risks of this type of research are equally clear. In laboratories where pathogens are manipulated or studied under artificial conditions, there is always a risk that an accident could result in a release. Even with the strictest safety measures, human error or equipment malfunction can lead to breaches. In 2014, for example, incidents involving anthrax and avian influenza in U.S. laboratories underscored the potential dangers associated with research facilities, even in highly controlled settings. These incidents, which thankfully did not result in outbreaks, highlighted how even seemingly minor lapses could escalate into serious public health threats. As a result, the potential for unintended consequences must be a constant consideration in research planning and execution.

The ethical dilemma at the heart of this issue revolves around the pursuit of knowledge versus the protection of public safety. Should scientists pursue research that could help us understand and potentially prevent pandemics, even if that research carries a small risk of accidentally creating one? Advocates for high-risk research argue that knowledge is power and that without exploring potential viral behaviors, humanity will remain vulnerable to future outbreaks. However, opponents of certain research methods, particularly gain-of-function studies where viruses are genetically altered to study their transmissibility or virulence, caution that the risks may outweigh the benefits. They argue that such studies could lead to unintended consequences with catastrophic results if safety protocols fail.

Compounding this challenge is the public's perception of high-stakes research. For many, the idea of intentionally manipulating pathogens in a laboratory environment is unsettling. This discomfort, combined with historical instances of accidental exposures, feeds skepticism about the necessity and safety of such studies. In particular, the COVID-19 pandemic has brought public scrutiny to the fore, with questions about lab safety, research motives, and scientific accountability dominating public discourse. Maintaining public trust is therefore essential, as any breach or accident could erode confidence in scientific institutions, leading to broader societal repercussions that hinder scientific progress.

In response to these concerns, some in the scientific community are calling for a reassessment of high-stakes research practices. Suggestions include increasing regulatory oversight, implementing stricter ethical guidelines, and establishing transparent frameworks that allow for independent audits of high-containment laboratories. There is also a push for greater public engagement in discussions about the potential risks and rewards of such research, to ensure that communities understand why it is conducted and how the risks are mitigated. Increased transparency could help bridge the gap between scientific institutions and the public, fostering a collaborative approach to addressing health threats.

In the end, the balance between innovation and risk in virology and other pathogen-related research is not a simple equation. It requires constant evaluation and recalibration, taking into account new scientific discoveries, emerging global health trends, and societal attitudes toward risk. By rigorously weighing the potential benefits against the risks and by implementing robust safety protocols, the scientific community can strive to harness the power of innovation responsibly. Through this balanced approach, researchers can work towards advancing knowledge that ultimately serves the greater good, while ensuring that public safety remains a top priority.

The Call for Global Standards and Collaborative Oversight

The COVID-19 pandemic underscored the urgent need for international cooperation and standards in managing biological research. While scientific knowledge knows no borders, the practices, safety protocols, and ethical considerations in high-stakes research vary widely from one country to another. As viruses and other pathogens do not adhere to political boundaries, neither can the guidelines meant to prevent their accidental or intentional release. To truly mitigate global risks, scientists, policymakers, and institutions worldwide must work together to establish consistent, rigorous standards that prioritize transparency, safety, and public accountability.

At the heart of the movement toward global standards is the need for universal protocols in biosafety and biosecurity. Laboratories that handle high-risk pathogens currently operate under a mix of national and institutional regulations, creating a fragmented approach to containment and safety. For example, while some countries mandate that all high-containment labs undergo periodic audits by independent experts, others rely solely on internal assessments. Without uniform regulations, gaps in safety practices emerge, increasing the potential for accidents. A comprehensive global framework could help harmonize these efforts, ensuring that all labs adhere to the same stringent safety measures, regardless of location.

The World Health Organization (WHO) has made strides in encouraging international dialogue on biosafety standards. By fostering conversations among nations, it aims to establish minimum safety protocols that all laboratories must follow. However, compliance remains voluntary, and enforcement is inconsistent. The lack of binding international agreements on lab safety not only poses a risk to public health but also weakens the trust between nations, as each country's security depends partially on the safety measures of others. Moving forward, binding agreements with clear accountability structures could enhance both safety and trust, setting a new precedent for how scientific risks are managed globally.

One significant proposal for strengthening international oversight is the establishment of an independent, global body that would be responsible for auditing and regulating high-containment labs worldwide. This body would ideally operate similarly to the International Atomic Energy Agency (IAEA), which monitors nuclear facilities to prevent misuse and ensure safety standards. An international agency dedicated to biosafety could play a similar role, conducting regular inspections, verifying compliance, and providing a transparent record of each facility's safety practices. Such a body would require widespread support and funding from member nations, but the potential benefits to global health security could be profound.

Furthermore, international collaboration in scientific research can strengthen oversight efforts. Cross-border research partnerships, which have become increasingly common, offer unique opportunities for scientists to share best practices, conduct joint assessments, and hold one another accountable. By encouraging and supporting collaborations between labs in different countries, the scientific community can foster a culture of safety that transcends national interests. Such collaborations also allow researchers to pool resources, share data more effectively, and address health threats from a holistic, global perspective rather than through the lens of national interest.

The call for global standards and collaborative oversight is also rooted in the ethical responsibility that comes with high-stakes research. As scientists push the boundaries of knowledge, particularly in virology and genetic engineering, they must be held to a level of accountability commensurate with the potential impact of their work. The public has a right to know that laboratories handling dangerous pathogens are being monitored rigorously and that scientists are operating with a commitment to the safety of all humanity. Enhanced transparency and standardized practices could help build public trust in scientific research, which is essential for maintaining support for potentially life-saving work.

In response to these calls, some countries are already taking steps to strengthen biosafety protocols. The United States, for instance, has expanded its regulatory requirements for facilities conducting research on pathogens with pandemic potential. In Europe, there are ongoing discussions about establishing more unified standards for biosafety across the EU member states. However, until these initiatives are part of a cohesive, global strategy, the risk of unequal enforcement and regulatory gaps will persist.

In conclusion, establishing global standards for biosafety and biosecurity is essential in today's interconnected world. By fostering collaboration, enhancing oversight, and promoting accountability, the international community can work towards a safer environment for conducting high-stakes research. While the journey toward comprehensive global oversight is challenging, the COVID-19 pandemic serves as a powerful reminder that when it comes to public health, the world is only as strong as its weakest link.

Chapter 11: Impact on Global Health Policies

Shifts in Pandemic Preparedness Plans

The COVID-19 pandemic exposed vulnerabilities in global pandemic preparedness and spurred health organizations, governments, and international coalitions to overhaul their approach to managing and preventing future pandemics. Theories around the origins of COVID-19—whether through zoonotic transmission, a lab leak, or a combination of factors—highlighted the need for improved detection, containment, and response strategies. As governments worldwide grappled with the devastating impacts of COVID-19, a consensus emerged on the necessity of more resilient, proactive, and adaptable pandemic preparedness plans.

Prior to COVID-19, pandemic plans in many countries were focused on influenza-like pathogens, with fewer provisions for unexpected, highly contagious viruses that may behave differently from traditional flu viruses. The theories regarding COVID-19's origins and the virus's unique characteristics led policymakers to expand the scope of preparedness plans to include a wider array of potential pathogens. Recognizing that pandemics may originate from natural sources or accidental releases from labs, health authorities began revising their protocols to consider more comprehensive scenarios. Plans now include enhanced response frameworks for high-containment labs, detailed response blueprints for pathogens with airborne and contact transmission routes, and protocols for rapidly scaling public health resources.

Central to these new plans is a stronger emphasis on early detection and swift containment. The global response to COVID-19 revealed significant gaps in the ability to identify and track novel pathogens before they spread widely. In response, many countries are investing in enhanced surveillance systems designed to identify unusual illness patterns among both humans and animals. These systems rely on data from hospitals, community clinics, and agricultural settings to create a comprehensive surveillance network. Additionally, countries are employing more advanced data analytics and artificial intelligence to detect anomalies in health trends, allowing for a faster and more accurate identification of potential pandemics.

The reallocation of resources has also been crucial to these revised preparedness plans. Prior to COVID-19, many countries struggled to maintain adequate stocks of personal protective equipment (PPE), ventilators, and other medical essentials. Learning from these challenges, governments have adopted a new approach to resource management. Many are now stockpiling critical items to prevent future shortages, while also establishing flexible production agreements with manufacturers. This allows for the rapid scaling up of essential goods in the event of another outbreak. Some nations have even created "pandemic reserve funds" to ensure that sufficient financial resources are immediately available for emergency use, streamlining funding access during crises.

Specific examples of revised pandemic plans highlight how different regions have adapted. The United States, for instance, expanded the capabilities of its Strategic National Stockpile to include a wider range of critical medical supplies, while also revising its criteria for when stockpiled resources can be deployed. The European Union has introduced new pandemic response policies that facilitate cross-border coordination, making it easier to distribute medical supplies and personnel where they are most needed. Meanwhile, Japan has implemented an extensive revision of its Infectious Disease Control Law, giving local and national authorities greater flexibility to respond swiftly to emerging health threats.

On a global scale, the World Health Organization (WHO) has stepped up efforts to lead collaborative pandemic preparedness initiatives, with a renewed focus on preventing lab-based outbreaks alongside natural pandemics. Through its Health Emergencies Programme, the WHO has enhanced its role in coordinating pandemic preparedness training and sharing resources among member states. It has also begun to work closely with national governments to support the implementation of these revised preparedness plans, ensuring that countries are better equipped to respond collaboratively to future pandemics.

Ultimately, these shifts in pandemic preparedness underscore a paradigm shift in public health: the focus has moved from reactionary measures to preventive and proactive strategies. While the COVID-19 pandemic took the world by surprise, the lessons learned from this experience have prompted a transformative approach to pandemic planning. By improving early detection, ensuring sufficient resources, and fostering international collaboration, health authorities aim to reduce the likelihood of another catastrophic pandemic and protect global health more effectively.

Revisions to Biosafety and Biosecurity Regulations

As theories surrounding the origins of COVID-19 gained international attention, a central focus turned to laboratory safety and the protocols governing research with potentially dangerous pathogens. The lab-leak theory, which suggested that COVID-19 might have escaped from a high-containment facility, heightened public awareness of biosecurity and underscored the importance of stringent regulations. This intensified scrutiny spurred a wave of changes in biosafety and biosecurity standards around the world. Governments and scientific institutions re-evaluated protocols to mitigate risks associated with pathogen research, especially in laboratories handling viruses capable of causing widespread human infections.

High-level biosafety laboratories, known as BSL-3 and BSL-4 labs, handle some of the world's most infectious and dangerous pathogens. These labs are required to implement strict containment measures and follow protocols to prevent accidental releases. Prior to the pandemic, guidelines for these facilities were comprehensive but varied significantly between countries, creating a patchwork of standards across the globe. The COVID-19 pandemic and its impact on public health led to renewed calls for international alignment on biosecurity measures, particularly among laboratories conducting "gain-of-function" research, which involves modifying pathogens to study their transmissibility or virulence. Gain-of-function research can offer crucial insights into how viruses evolve, but it also poses inherent risks if containment protocols fail.

To address these concerns, several countries have introduced more rigorous biosecurity regulations aimed at strengthening safety protocols in high-containment labs. In the United States, for instance, the Centers for Disease Control and Prevention (CDC) and the National Institutes of Health (NIH) have enhanced the oversight of gain-of-function research. New rules mandate more comprehensive risk assessments, regular inspections, and clear lines of accountability for laboratory personnel. The U.S. has also established a higher threshold for approving such research, requiring scientists to demonstrate the absolute necessity of gain-of-function experiments and to provide detailed plans for risk mitigation.

Similarly, in Europe, the European Union's European Centre for Disease Prevention and Control (ECDC) has ramped up its biosecurity framework, aligning standards across member states to ensure a unified approach. New guidelines include more frequent audits of BSL-3 and BSL-4 laboratories and stricter requirements for reporting laboratory accidents or protocol breaches. These updates aim to improve transparency, enabling the public and policymakers to understand the potential risks associated with pathogen research and fostering a culture of accountability within research institutions.

In China, where the Wuhan Institute of Virology (WIV) has been at the center of COVID-19 origin theories, the government has taken substantial steps to fortify its biosafety regulations. The Chinese Ministry of Science and Technology issued sweeping reforms aimed at standardizing biosafety measures across all high-containment labs. These include mandatory training programs for lab workers, enhanced protocols for waste management, and increased oversight by regulatory bodies. In addition, Chinese authorities have mandated that all pathogen research projects undergo rigorous ethical and safety reviews prior to approval, with greater scrutiny on experiments involving novel coronaviruses.

Internationally, the World Health Organization (WHO) has been working to develop a global biosafety and biosecurity framework that would establish uniform standards for laboratories worldwide. Recognizing the importance of a coordinated approach, the WHO has called on member states to adopt common safety protocols and reporting mechanisms. This initiative aims to ensure that even the most stringent standards are met universally, reducing the risk of accidental pathogen releases and fostering global trust in the research community. Part of this effort involves creating an international task force that regularly inspects high-containment labs and offers resources for training and compliance.

These regulatory changes represent a significant shift in how the world approaches biosecurity and lab safety. The increased oversight and stringent protocols underscore a shared commitment to balancing scientific exploration with public safety. For scientists, these updates provide a clearer framework within which to conduct their research responsibly, while also addressing public concerns about the potential hazards of pathogen research. By implementing these enhanced biosafety and biosecurity regulations, governments and institutions hope to ensure that research facilities are equipped to prevent accidental releases and that scientists are held to the highest standards of accountability.

At its core, the revision of biosafety and biosecurity regulations reflects a new era of responsibility and awareness in the scientific community. By learning from the challenges and uncertainties of the COVID-19 pandemic, nations worldwide are working to create a safer and more transparent environment for vital research on infectious diseases. These developments mark a positive step toward securing the future of public health, as scientists continue their efforts to better understand the complex and evolving world of pathogens.

Re-evaluating International Research Collaboration

The COVID-19 pandemic highlighted the significance of international cooperation in scientific research, especially in addressing global health crises. However, the pandemic also exposed the vulnerabilities in these collaborations, revealing how political tensions and mistrust between countries can impact joint research efforts. As debates over COVID-19's origins intensified, collaborative projects in virology and epidemiology came under increased scrutiny, with many countries calling for stricter guidelines to govern international partnerships in sensitive areas of research.

One prominent example of international cooperation in pathogen research is the relationship between the United States and China, both leaders in virology research with extensive networks of collaboration prior to the pandemic. American institutions, including the National Institutes of Health (NIH), had funded various research projects with the Wuhan Institute of Virology (WIV) as part of efforts to understand emerging infectious diseases, particularly coronaviruses. This partnership, like many others, was initially motivated by the global need to prevent future pandemics through shared research and pooled resources. However, as questions about the origins of COVID-19 emerged, so did concerns about the transparency and safety of these collaborations. Allegations surrounding the Wuhan lab, whether substantiated or not, have led many countries to reconsider the terms of their scientific partnerships, especially in fields involving pathogens with pandemic potential.

In response to these concerns, several countries and organizations have initiated efforts to establish new, more transparent protocols for international research collaborations. These measures emphasize the importance of data-sharing, transparency, and mutual accountability among partner institutions. For instance, the United States has implemented more stringent requirements for U.S.-funded research conducted abroad, mandating that all foreign research partners adhere to U.S. biosafety standards, particularly for high-risk pathogen research. These updated guidelines are designed to ensure that the same level of oversight and safety is applied internationally, reducing the potential for inconsistencies that could lead to public mistrust.

Meanwhile, Europe has also introduced a new framework aimed at promoting transparency in international research partnerships. The European Union's new protocols require that any foreign entity collaborating on EU-funded research projects submit to regular audits and public reporting of their biosafety practices. These measures are intended to ensure that European research standards are upheld regardless of where the research takes place, fostering an environment of accountability and transparency that is consistent across borders.

China, in turn, has responded to the increased scrutiny by enhancing its own regulations on foreign-funded research projects, particularly those involving pathogens. Chinese authorities have introduced additional review mechanisms for projects involving international partners, with an emphasis on research ethics, data-sharing policies, and biosafety compliance. The Chinese government has also implemented stricter guidelines for joint publications, requiring that all research findings undergo thorough review by national scientific bodies before they are released publicly. These changes are intended to address both international concerns and the Chinese public's own desire for accountability in sensitive areas of research.

The World Health Organization (WHO) has also taken steps to facilitate safer and more transparent international research collaborations. Recognizing the value of global teamwork in preventing future pandemics, the WHO has proposed a series of international standards for collaborative research, including protocols for data-sharing, biosafety, and emergency response planning. These recommendations encourage countries to adopt consistent practices that prioritize both scientific advancement and public safety. To enforce these standards, the WHO is working on establishing a monitoring body that would assess the compliance of research institutions worldwide with these new protocols, ensuring that all participants in global health research adhere to rigorous standards.

While these changes mark a significant shift toward safer and more accountable scientific partnerships, they also present new challenges. Stricter regulations and increased oversight may create additional administrative burdens for researchers, potentially slowing down the pace of discovery and limiting the scope of international collaboration. Additionally, countries may find it difficult to balance national interests with global transparency, particularly in fields with national security implications. As a result, there is an ongoing debate within the scientific community about how to foster trust in international research while safeguarding sensitive information and adhering to the necessary biosecurity protocols.

Despite these challenges, the re-evaluation of international research collaboration is a vital step toward creating a more resilient and transparent global health landscape. By addressing the gaps exposed during the COVID-19 pandemic, these new measures aim to restore public confidence in scientific research and ensure that international partnerships are conducted responsibly. Ultimately, these reforms represent a shared commitment among nations to prioritize safety, transparency, and accountability in the pursuit of scientific knowledge. As the world continues to grapple with the lasting effects of COVID-19, these updated protocols for international collaboration may play a crucial role in preparing humanity for future health challenges.

Strengthening Biosafety Standards and Laboratory Protocols

The COVID-19 pandemic brought global attention to the protocols governing biosafety standards and laboratory practices, particularly in facilities researching dangerous pathogens. With increased scrutiny surrounding COVID-19's origins, especially regarding the potential lab-leak theory, the need to re-evaluate and reinforce biosafety protocols has become a focal point for governments and research institutions worldwide. The goal is to ensure that future scientific endeavors involving high-risk pathogens are conducted with the utmost safety, accountability, and transparency.

One of the primary concerns raised during the pandemic was the oversight of laboratories classified as Biosafety Level 3 (BSL-3) and Biosafety Level 4 (BSL-4), where the world's most hazardous pathogens are studied. These facilities are designed to handle organisms that pose a high risk to both laboratory personnel and the public, requiring stringent safety measures to prevent accidental exposure or release. Despite these safeguards, several incidents involving accidental pathogen release have occurred over the years, which has fueled calls for strengthening current protocols. These incidents, along with the heightened focus on the Wuhan Institute of Virology, underscore the need for even more comprehensive biosafety measures in facilities handling infectious agents.

In response to these concerns, countries around the world have implemented new protocols to bolster laboratory safety. In the United States, the National Institutes of Health (NIH) and the Centers for Disease Control and Prevention (CDC) have updated their guidelines, mandating additional layers of oversight for research involving pathogens with pandemic potential. This includes regular audits, mandatory safety training, and increased accountability for lab personnel. Furthermore, the U.S. government has introduced new funding requirements that tie research grants to stringent biosafety compliance, encouraging research facilities to adopt the highest possible standards of safety. Laboratories failing to meet these standards may face funding cuts or even be prohibited from conducting certain types of research, emphasizing a shift toward a zero-tolerance approach regarding biosafety breaches.

In Europe, similar measures have been enacted as part of the European Union's revised biosecurity framework. European laboratories handling high-risk pathogens are now required to undergo more frequent inspections, with the results made available to both government agencies and the public. The EU has also implemented new policies requiring labs to report any potential biosafety lapses to regulatory authorities immediately, enabling faster responses to contain any potential threats. These regulations emphasize transparency and public accountability, aiming to build public trust in the handling of infectious agents while reducing the likelihood of accidental releases.

China has also taken significant steps to reinforce laboratory safety in response to international and domestic concerns. The Chinese government introduced new regulations mandating a certification process for researchers working in BSL-3 and BSL-4 labs, ensuring that only those with extensive training and experience handle dangerous pathogens. Additionally, Chinese authorities have increased oversight over domestic research involving zoonotic viruses, focusing on potential spillover risks from animal to human populations. The government has committed to conducting periodic inspections of high-level biosafety labs, with an emphasis on compliance with international safety standards. This renewed focus on biosecurity highlights China's recognition of the global responsibility associated with researching potentially dangerous pathogens.

The World Health Organization (WHO) has played an instrumental role in coordinating international efforts to update biosafety standards. Recognizing the global nature of biosecurity risks, the WHO has issued a new set of guidelines designed to create a baseline for biosafety protocols worldwide. These recommendations include standards for facility construction, training requirements, and emergency response protocols, all aimed at minimizing the risks associated with handling infectious agents. The WHO has also established a new oversight body to monitor compliance with these guidelines, offering resources and support for laboratories seeking to enhance their biosafety practices. By promoting a standardized approach to laboratory safety, the WHO hopes to mitigate the potential for accidents across international borders.

One of the significant advancements in biosafety has been the adoption of enhanced containment technologies. Innovations such as advanced ventilation systems, automated pathogen-handling equipment, and real-time environmental monitoring tools are helping to reduce human interaction with dangerous pathogens, thereby minimizing the risk of accidental exposure. Research facilities in many countries are now incorporating these technologies into their design, creating a safer working environment for scientists and reducing the likelihood of pathogen escape. In addition, improvements in digital tracking and security measures allow for more precise monitoring of pathogen samples, ensuring that research materials are strictly accounted for and accessible only to authorized personnel.

While these developments represent progress in biosafety, challenges remain in implementing and maintaining these standards globally. Differences in resources and technological capabilities mean that not all countries can meet the highest standards, creating potential vulnerabilities. To address this, wealthier nations and international organizations have been encouraged to provide funding and technical support to labs in developing countries, helping them reach a level of safety comparable to that of their more advanced counterparts. Additionally, disparities in regulatory enforcement can create gaps in the biosecurity landscape, necessitating ongoing dialogue and cooperation between nations to ensure a cohesive approach to biosafety.

Strengthening biosafety standards and laboratory protocols is not just a matter of preventing accidental releases but also of reinforcing public confidence in scientific research. The COVID-19 pandemic has underscored the profound impact that a pathogen can have on societies and economies, highlighting the need for robust safeguards in pathogen research. By ensuring that laboratories operate under the highest standards of safety and accountability, governments and scientific communities can reassure the public that pathogen research is conducted responsibly, with minimal risk to public health.

Ultimately, the global commitment to improving biosafety standards represents a collective effort to mitigate the risks associated with studying dangerous pathogens. As new viruses continue to emerge and the potential for pandemics remains an ever-present threat, these enhanced protocols are essential in building a safer and more resilient global research environment. The lessons learned from COVID-19 serve as a reminder of the importance of vigilance, transparency, and innovation in laboratory safety, guiding future research efforts toward a model that prioritizes both scientific advancement and the welfare of humanity.

Future Implications for International Health Governance and Biosecurity

As COVID-19 reshapes the world's approach to health security, the need for robust international health governance has become apparent. Global biosecurity is no longer an isolated concern; it is central to preventing future pandemics and managing emerging health threats. The pandemic underscored both the limitations and the potential of international health organizations like the World Health Organization (WHO) in coordinating global responses. It also brought attention to the importance of effective communication, transparency, and cooperation between countries to safeguard public health worldwide.

Historically, health security has been largely national in scope, with countries implementing their own measures to contain health crises. However, COVID-19 revealed that infectious diseases transcend borders, underscoring the necessity for unified global responses to biosecurity threats. This shared need has led to a reevaluation of international health governance structures, with policymakers and public health experts advocating for stronger frameworks to facilitate cooperation. Central to this is the idea of a legally binding global biosecurity treaty, which would mandate nations to adhere to specific standards for pathogen research, laboratory safety, and data sharing in real time.

The proposed biosecurity treaty would serve multiple functions. First, it would establish a set of baseline protocols for biosafety and biosecurity, ensuring that countries with varying levels of research capacity adhere to globally accepted standards. This includes standardizing laboratory protocols for handling infectious agents and implementing mandatory safety audits. Such protocols would not only improve safety in labs globally but also establish a framework for mutual accountability. Secondly, the treaty would emphasize early detection and rapid response mechanisms, allowing nations to alert others promptly about outbreaks with pandemic potential. Building trust is a critical factor here; countries may hesitate to report new diseases due to fears of economic or political backlash. A well-structured treaty could mitigate these concerns by creating a framework for transparent communication without punitive repercussions, promoting more honest and timely reporting of health threats.

Another potential aspect of the treaty is the creation of an independent oversight body tasked with monitoring global adherence to biosecurity measures. The oversight body, separate from existing organizations like the WHO, would ensure that biosafety regulations are being followed and that labs engaged in high-risk pathogen research meet international standards. This independent entity would also conduct investigations in the event of significant breaches or pandemics, ideally eliminating the risk of political biases or conflicts of interest. By conducting assessments and making recommendations, this oversight body would aim to maintain high biosecurity standards and prevent accidental or intentional misuse of biological agents. The impartial nature of this body would be crucial to its credibility, as it would be tasked with mediating sensitive issues that often span national interests and global welfare.

An equally important aspect of improved biosecurity governance is data sharing. The pandemic highlighted delays in the sharing of genetic data, which hindered global understanding of COVID-19's spread and mutation patterns. A comprehensive biosecurity treaty would need to mandate real-time data sharing and provide clear protocols for handling sensitive genetic information. Recent technological advances, such as blockchain, could enable secure and transparent data exchanges that protect sensitive information while allowing researchers worldwide to access critical data quickly. Open-source data platforms could also facilitate collaboration, enabling scientists to track virus evolution in real time, identify hotspots, and develop more effective vaccines or treatments.

Funding for biosecurity initiatives remains a pressing issue. Many lower-income nations lack the resources needed to implement high-level biosafety protocols or conduct research into emerging pathogens. The international community has recognized this disparity, and many experts argue that funding mechanisms should be embedded within the framework of a global biosecurity treaty. Wealthier nations and international organizations, such as the United Nations and the G7, could contribute to a dedicated biosecurity fund. This fund would be allocated to support infrastructure development, laboratory upgrades, and personnel training in lower-income nations, ensuring that even the most resource-limited countries can meet baseline biosafety and biosecurity standards. Such equitable distribution of resources would not only improve global preparedness but also foster greater cooperation and solidarity among nations.

Global health crises like COVID-19 have shown that even the most robust treaty or regulatory framework must account for rapid adaptation. This flexibility could be built into international governance structures by creating "emergency clauses" that would activate in the event of a pandemic or other high-risk biological event. These clauses could include temporary adjustments to research protocols, fast-tracking of containment measures, and mandatory information-sharing mandates. Such measures could be critical in rapidly deploying medical countermeasures and coordinating responses in the face of unpredictable, fast-moving threats. By creating adaptable frameworks, international governance can balance stability with responsiveness, ensuring preparedness for novel threats that may emerge in unforeseen ways.

Implementing a comprehensive international biosecurity framework will require collaboration, trust-building, and the gradual alignment of diverse national interests. However, the benefits of such an endeavor are immense. A strengthened system of global health governance would not only help prevent future pandemics but would also serve as a model for addressing other transnational health challenges, from antimicrobial resistance to climate-driven zoonotic disease outbreaks.

Ultimately, establishing effective biosecurity governance through collaborative treaties, independent oversight, and fair funding structures has implications far beyond managing infectious diseases. It is a vital step toward building a more resilient global community, one that recognizes the interconnected nature of public health and understands that the security of one nation impacts the security of all. The COVID-19 pandemic has served as a reminder of the power of pathogens to shape our world and has opened a new chapter in our collective commitment to health security.

Chapter 12: Conclusion

Summarizing Key Points

As we reach the conclusion of this book, it is essential to revisit the key areas explored throughout, which encompass a range of theories, perspectives, and debates surrounding the origin of COVID-19. Understanding the pandemic's beginnings is a profound endeavor that extends beyond scientific curiosity and touches upon global health, ethics, politics, and public trust.

At the outset, we explored the introduction of COVID-19 into the global landscape, recognizing its swift and unprecedented impact. The early chapters delved into the widespread disruptions that COVID-19 caused worldwide, impacting economies, altering lives, and shifting public discourse. A significant part of understanding this virus's origin involves examining the compelling reasons for which knowing its roots matters—whether it was a naturally occurring zoonotic spillover or a result of human involvement. The ramifications of each theory have direct implications for biosecurity and the prevention of future pandemics.

We then ventured into the historical context of biological weapons, understanding the foundation of fears surrounding laboratory work with potentially dangerous pathogens. This historical context revealed that humanity's experience with weaponized pathogens dates back centuries, with various governments and groups utilizing biological agents to achieve their goals. This part of our examination underscored that public apprehension toward biological research isn't unfounded. Although COVID-19 itself has not been classified as a biological weapon, the historical lessons remain relevant, helping contextualize why many have questioned the virus's origins.

Moving into the specifics, we explored the Wuhan Institute of Virology (WIV), a globally recognized laboratory dedicated to studying infectious diseases. With its involvement in researching coronaviruses and its proximity to the outbreak's epicenter, the WIV has been at the heart of speculations and theories. This examination provided insight into the lab's operations, its research on coronaviruses, and the theories suggesting that COVID-19 may have accidentally leaked from this institution. At the same time, we considered the lab's safety measures, protocols, and the statements from scientists and governments worldwide who argue in support of its integrity.

In contrast to the lab-leak theory, the natural origin theory presents COVID-19 as a zoonotic virus, one that jumped from animals to humans through natural means. Here, we explored the scientific evidence for natural zoonotic transmission, including comparisons with previous coronavirus outbreaks like SARS and MERS. The natural origin theory has substantial backing among the scientific community, given the established precedent of animal-to-human virus transmissions. However, even within this theory, questions remain, particularly around how, when, and where the virus may have jumped species before making its way into human populations.

As we reviewed each theory, the narrative was consistently influenced by political reactions, media coverage, and public perception. The role of politics was particularly notable, affecting how different governments approached the investigation and communicated with their citizens. Some political entities, such as the United States and China, engaged in diplomatic sparring over the virus's origins, with their positions and statements influencing public and international attitudes. Media coverage, in turn, often reflected these polarized views, shaping the global understanding of COVID-19 and adding to the spread of theories and counter-theories. Public reactions varied widely, and misinformation flourished, complicating the already difficult task of finding consensus on the virus's origins.

In this summary, it's clear that each perspective explored in this book has merit and has contributed to our broader understanding of COVID-19's origins. The search for answers remains an ongoing journey, as scientists, political leaders, and the public continue to navigate the complex intersections of health, ethics, and science. As we move forward, the lessons learned from these explorations remind us that, beyond discovering COVID-19's exact origin, there is a broader imperative to strengthen our resilience against future pandemics and to commit ourselves to transparency, ethical standards, and global collaboration in the pursuit of truth.

Importance of Uncovering the Truth

The significance of uncovering COVID-19's true origin goes beyond resolving a scientific mystery. Pinpointing the beginnings of a pandemic that disrupted the entire world carries profound implications for public health, international relations, scientific integrity, and global preparedness. Each theory—whether the virus emerged naturally or through a lab incident—provides distinct lessons that can inform how we respond to future pandemics. But more than that, the pursuit of truth is essential in rebuilding public trust in science, ensuring accountability, and improving global collaboration in the face of health crises.

A core reason for understanding the virus's origins is pandemic preparedness. If COVID-19 arose from a zoonotic transmission, it would add urgency to monitoring and regulating wildlife interactions and habitats, especially in regions where human and animal boundaries overlap. Such knowledge could drive policies to restrict wildlife trade, enhance sanitation in live animal markets, and minimize human encroachment into natural habitats. Countries would need to prioritize surveillance of potential zoonotic pathogens and improve data sharing on emerging viruses. However, if the virus originated from a lab accident, it would call for an entirely different response. In this scenario, the focus would shift toward enforcing stricter safety protocols, enhancing oversight in research labs, and implementing rigorous international standards for research on potentially dangerous pathogens.

Beyond preparation, public trust hinges on transparency. From the beginning, the pandemic has strained public confidence in institutions, as conflicting narratives and information eroded belief in reliable sources. By actively pursuing and disclosing all that is known about COVID-19's origin, governments and scientific organizations can help restore credibility and faith in global health institutions. Transparency is particularly important because it underscores a commitment to truth over any geopolitical or economic interests. When institutions prioritize openness and allow research findings to emerge freely, they demonstrate integrity and accountability—qualities that are indispensable in times of global crisis.

Understanding the origins of COVID-19 also has implications for ethical standards in scientific research. Whether or not this pandemic originated from a lab, the very possibility has brought bioethical questions to the forefront. Is it responsible to conduct research that involves gain-of-function experiments on highly infectious pathogens? Are the current global protocols around such research sufficient? The importance of these ethical considerations is magnified when research involves potential risks that could endanger public health on a massive scale. As scientific progress advances, so too must the ethical frameworks that guide it, ensuring that innovation does not outpace our ability to manage its consequences responsibly.

International relations have also felt the strain from the uncertainty surrounding COVID-19's origin. Diplomatic tensions, particularly between the United States and China, have underscored how geopolitics can complicate scientific inquiries and undermine cooperative efforts. Determining the virus's origin could either confirm or dispel suspicions, potentially easing or exacerbating global political tensions. Regardless of the outcome, the experience highlights the need for a globally coordinated approach to disease prevention—one that is shielded from national agendas. Without transparent, apolitical collaboration, the world risks allowing future pandemics to become tools in diplomatic and ideological struggles rather than shared challenges to overcome.

In a broader sense, uncovering the truth about COVID-19's origin serves as a means of holding institutions accountable. Governments, research labs, and health organizations are all accountable to the public for their actions, whether those involve research practices or crisis management. The pandemic has exposed cracks in global health systems and revealed areas where responsibility must be taken seriously to prevent avoidable disasters. By finding the truth and learning from it, we set a precedent for transparency and responsibility that will make a critical difference in protecting future generations.

The importance of understanding COVID-19's origins is not just about assigning blame or confirming theories; it's about ensuring we learn from this experience to forge a safer, healthier future. The lessons drawn from this pursuit will inform every level of public health policy, scientific integrity, and international cooperation. Ultimately, finding the truth is about resilience: the resilience of systems, institutions, and humanity itself in the face of crisis. The ongoing journey to uncover COVID-19's beginnings symbolizes a commitment to truth that transcends any one nation, organization, or theory, underscoring a collective responsibility to protect and prepare for the world of tomorrow.

Early Challenges and Obstacles to Uncovering the Truth

From the outset, efforts to investigate COVID-19's origins faced significant challenges, ranging from logistical hurdles to political barriers, and at times, outright resistance. These early obstacles were not only due to the virus's rapid spread, which initially demanded all resources be directed toward managing the pandemic, but also due to the charged political environment surrounding the virus's origin. The combination of scientific, bureaucratic, and diplomatic challenges slowed early investigations, complicating efforts to piece together the story of how COVID-19 first entered the human population.

One of the primary hurdles was the urgent need to respond to the rapidly evolving health crisis itself. In early 2020, the virus spread at a speed that overwhelmed health systems, demanding immediate action to mitigate the impact rather than an exhaustive investigation into its origins. Health organizations, scientists, and governments were heavily invested in controlling the outbreak, providing care to infected patients, developing vaccines, and instituting public health protocols. This immediate crisis response was necessary to prevent further devastation but inadvertently postponed in-depth research into where and how the virus originated. It was only after the initial shock of the outbreak subsided that organizations could allocate attention to understanding its source.

Additionally, the need for international cooperation complicated the situation. Investigating the origin of a pandemic requires collaboration across borders, sharing sensitive data, and conducting joint fieldwork in the virus's early epicenter. But international cooperation was hindered by a lack of transparency and delays in sharing critical information. In the case of COVID-19, these challenges were evident as tensions rose between major global powers, most notably the United States and China. Each country's approach to transparency and data-sharing affected the speed and scope of the investigation. Meanwhile, the politicization of COVID-19's origins led to accusations and suspicions on both sides, with some officials and media outlets framing the virus's origin as an instrument of blame or political leverage rather than a public health question. This adversarial atmosphere discouraged openness and made cooperation more challenging at a time when it was most needed.

There were also scientific obstacles to consider, as finding a definitive answer about COVID-19's origins is scientifically complex. Determining the origin of a virus requires meticulous collection of data, including samples from potential animal reservoirs, genetic analyses, and environmental studies of areas where early cases were concentrated. In cases of zoonotic viruses, this process often involves tracing genetic similarities to known coronaviruses in animals, especially those in close proximity to human activity. However, in COVID-19's case, even with extensive studies on bats and other wildlife, the virus's exact source remains elusive. Gathering samples that can conclusively link the virus to a natural or lab source has proven to be an immense scientific challenge, compounded by the logistical difficulties in accessing and analyzing samples that may have deteriorated over time.

Beyond logistical and scientific barriers, there were institutional hurdles within global health organizations. Early on, the World Health Organization (WHO) attempted to coordinate an investigation into COVID-19's origins, but their mission faced several limitations, from restrictions on field access to limitations on available data. The WHO's efforts to investigate in China involved negotiation and compromise, and the organization was often criticized for not being assertive enough in its approach. Political sensitivities limited the WHO's reach and authority, as it had to work within the diplomatic confines of each country's regulations. Despite efforts to form an independent and balanced investigative team, the WHO struggled to balance scientific inquiry with maintaining political neutrality. These early struggles within such organizations exemplified the tension between science and diplomacy, further slowing the search for COVID-19's origins.

Public mistrust also grew as obstacles mounted, further complicating the search for answers. As news emerged of delays and limited access, some segments of the public began questioning the transparency and credibility of the investigation itself. This mistrust was amplified by the spread of misinformation and conspiracy theories online, as well as inconsistent statements from public health and political leaders. The lack of clear, accessible information led to a gap that was often filled with speculation, leading to polarized public opinion. This mistrust put additional pressure on global health organizations and governments, who now not only had to navigate the logistical and scientific hurdles of an origin investigation but also contend with managing public perceptions and addressing widespread skepticism.

The early days of the search for COVID-19's origins were marked by a combination of logistical, political, and scientific barriers. While many of these challenges were unique to the specific circumstances of COVID-19, they underscored a broader issue in global health and pandemic preparedness. Understanding these obstacles highlights the need for stronger frameworks for international collaboration, greater transparency from institutions, and robust scientific methodologies that can adapt to high-stakes situations. These early setbacks reveal how complex and multifaceted the search for truth can be, especially in a global crisis where scientific and political interests intersect. By acknowledging these challenges, we gain insight into the urgency and importance of finding solutions that can prevent similar obstacles in future pandemic investigations.

Early International Investigations and Their Challenges

As the initial shock of the pandemic waned, international attention increasingly focused on uncovering the origins of COVID-19. Understanding where and how the virus originated was critical to preventing future outbreaks, improving biosecurity, and restoring public confidence. Governments and organizations around the world began to initiate investigations, often looking to cooperate with local and global health authorities to trace the virus's roots. However, these investigations faced formidable obstacles, ranging from limited access to critical data to political sensitivities that complicated fieldwork. This section examines the primary investigations that sought to uncover the truth behind COVID-19's origins, as well as the diplomatic, logistical, and scientific challenges that often impeded these efforts.

In early 2021, the World Health Organization (WHO) launched one of the first comprehensive international investigations into the origins of COVID-19. This mission, comprised of a team of scientists from around the world, was given the monumental task of visiting Wuhan, China—the location of the first known outbreak. The team aimed to conduct field studies, review data from hospitals and laboratories, and assess evidence that might indicate either a natural or lab-based origin. Although the WHO team was granted access to key locations, such as the Wuhan Institute of Virology and Huanan Seafood Market, their mission was constrained by both time and political limitations.

One of the central challenges of the WHO investigation was the scope and depth of data access. While the team was permitted to interview local scientists and review laboratory protocols, they had limited access to raw data, such as patient records and detailed environmental samples from the earliest days of the outbreak. Much of the data had either been destroyed or rendered unavailable by the time the investigation began, leaving critical gaps in the timeline of events. Some team members voiced concerns that the evidence they reviewed was insufficient to draw firm conclusions, given that they could not directly access key data from local laboratories or verify information independently. Consequently, the WHO's findings, which leaned toward a natural origin, were met with mixed reactions. Many experts felt that without more comprehensive access, any conclusions drawn would be inconclusive at best, leaving the world still uncertain about COVID-19's precise origins.

The WHO investigation also faced political hurdles that underscored the sensitive nature of the inquiry. From the beginning, China insisted that any investigation into COVID-19's origins must respect its sovereignty, requiring the WHO to negotiate terms that balanced investigative needs with diplomatic protocol. As a result, the WHO team's movements were sometimes restricted, and certain documents were available only in summary format, limiting the depth of analysis. The political pressures surrounding the investigation intensified when international leaders, particularly from the

United States, publicly called for a more rigorous inquiry into the lab-leak theory. These calls fueled tensions with China, which accused other nations of politicizing the pandemic. Consequently, diplomatic tensions slowed the WHO's progress and cast doubt on the impartiality of their findings, as some perceived the investigation as being unduly influenced by political constraints.

In response to these limitations, several countries initiated their own independent inquiries. The United States, for example, commissioned its intelligence agencies to investigate the origins of COVID-19, with a particular focus on the possibility of a lab-based origin. However, these investigations faced similar challenges, as Chinese authorities were reluctant to cooperate with any external investigation not sanctioned by their government. U.S. intelligence agencies reviewed existing genomic data, epidemiological evidence, and communication records from early in the pandemic but found themselves limited to circumstantial evidence. With no direct access to on-site data in Wuhan, their findings remained speculative, and the debate over COVID-19's origins continued to divide experts. These investigations illustrated the difficulty of probing another country's public health infrastructure, particularly when pandemic origins are entwined with matters of national security and scientific reputation.

International debates surrounding the origins of COVID-19 reflected a broader pattern of global mistrust, further exacerbated by the spread of misinformation and conspiracy theories. Many leaders argued that without a transparent investigation, public suspicion would grow, fueling theories that the virus had been deliberately concealed or mishandled. The absence of definitive answers allowed various origin theories to proliferate, from zoonotic spillover to bioweapon conspiracy claims, which complicated efforts to reach a global consensus on COVID-19's origin story. Public demand for accountability led to heightened scrutiny of global health protocols and the transparency of governments, further challenging institutions like the WHO to maintain neutrality amid a polarized information landscape.

Adding to the complexity were logistical barriers to conducting effective investigations. The Huanan Seafood Market, one of the first suspected sites of viral spread, had been thoroughly disinfected before international teams could collect detailed environmental samples, potentially erasing valuable clues. Similarly, some potential animal reservoirs in the area had either migrated or died, making it difficult to track the virus's movement through wildlife populations. The logistical challenges of tracing the virus through multiple species in one of the world's most densely populated regions made any investigation extraordinarily complex. Even with extensive collaboration, definitive evidence remained elusive, underscoring the daunting nature of tracing zoonotic spillover events or a lab breach.

These early international investigations ultimately highlighted the difficulty of obtaining concrete answers in the face of political, logistical, and scientific obstacles. They underscored the need for transparent, globally coordinated response systems that can swiftly investigate emerging infectious diseases without compromising due diligence or international relations. The lack of conclusive findings from the WHO and other national investigations left many unanswered questions but also spurred calls for improved preparedness and transparency protocols. In the absence of definitive answers, the early days of COVID-19's investigation stand as a testament to both the complexity of pandemic tracing and the profound impact of geopolitical dynamics on scientific inquiry. The lessons from these investigations will likely shape future approaches to international health crises, emphasizing the importance of global collaboration, prompt data sharing, and political neutrality in times of unprece-dented scientific challenges.

Ongoing Challenges and Future Directions

As the COVID-19 pandemic stretched into its later phases, the search for the virus's origin faced mounting challenges, some famil-iar and others unprecedented. While the initial investigations by in-ternational organizations and independent research bodies yielded insights, they left many questions unanswered. Limited access to on-the-ground data, national interests in controlling the narrative, and a lingering mistrust between countries continued to complicate efforts. Moving forward, scientists and global health organizations identified new methods and approaches to help secure a more de-finitive answer while also preparing for potential future pandemics. This section delves into the enduring barriers to investigation, the evolving methodologies in tracing virus origins, and the essential steps for improving pandemic response infrastructure.

One of the primary obstacles in determining COVID-19's ori-gins has been limited access to critical data. Many laboratories and health agencies in China and other nations faced heavy restrictions on what information could be publicly shared. Some of this was dri-ven by legitimate concerns over privacy and data protection; how-ever, much of it reflected the desire to avoid scrutiny and minimize political fallout. Certain information, such as raw patient data from the earliest cases and detailed lab records from facilities like the Wuhan Institute of Virology, has yet to be fully accessible to inter-national experts. The lack of direct access creates a significant bot-tleneck in understanding not only COVID-19 but also potential pathways for other zoonotic viruses to jump to humans.

In response to these challenges, many in the scientific community have advocated for the creation of more open data-sharing platforms and cooperative research hubs that prioritize transparency. For example, the Global Initiative on Sharing All Influenza Data (GISAID) offers a framework that enables countries to share viral sequence data in real time, a model that could be expanded for other infectious diseases. Experts argue that if similar systems were in place from the outset, critical data gaps could be closed, allowing for a more unified global response to the next pandemic. Such open platforms could also help to streamline communication between health organizations, research institutes, and government agencies. In turn, this could make data more readily available for tracing virus origins in real-time and pave the way for collaborative scientific studies to better identify potential sources of zoonotic spillover.

Advances in technology have also presented new methods for investigating viral origins. Genetic sequencing techniques, bioinformatics tools, and predictive models now enable researchers to analyze virus samples in extraordinary detail. These tools allow scientists to pinpoint small variations in the genetic makeup of a virus, track mutations, and build evolutionary trees to understand how a virus may have spread. With these techniques, it's possible to compare COVID-19 to other coronaviruses in animal reservoirs more effectively, offering clues to whether the virus originated from a wild animal, an intermediate host, or even laboratory research samples. If applied in a coordinated international effort, these technological advancements could provide a far more comprehensive picture of how viral transmissions unfold across species and regions.

However, these tools are only as effective as the data they rely on, bringing us back to the need for improved transparency and international cooperation. Without the cooperation of all countries involved in the initial outbreak, the full utility of genetic tools and data platforms cannot be realized. This reality has led to a renewed push for legal frameworks that mandate the sharing of key data during health crises. The WHO and other global health organizations are in discussions about policies that would require countries to provide access to samples and health data, albeit with protections to respect sovereignty and personal privacy. By standardizing international protocols for health crisis management, scientists and policymakers hope to foster a more unified approach to addressing and preventing pandemics.

In addition to data-sharing and technological advancements, strengthening global health systems remains essential to tracing viral origins and protecting populations against future pandemics. Many countries, particularly in low- and middle-income regions, still lack the infrastructure necessary to detect emerging viruses or respond swiftly to outbreaks. To address these disparities, international efforts have focused on building capacity through funding, training, and resource-sharing initiatives. The G7, G20, and other global alliances have prioritized investments in health systems, aiming to strengthen laboratory networks, improve diagnostic capabilities, and enhance disease surveillance in under-resourced regions. Through such efforts, the global community aims to better prepare for future outbreaks and create a reliable first line of defense against the next potential pandemic.

Despite these efforts, a crucial question remains: Will the lessons learned from COVID-19 lead to permanent improvements in global health security, or will the urgency fade as the pandemic recedes? History suggests that significant public health investments are often reactionary, with funding and political will waning once an immediate crisis is resolved. To counteract this, experts have proposed establishing independent pandemic preparedness agencies that operate year-round, similar to organizations like the CDC, which monitor and respond to potential threats regardless of current conditions. This would enable health organizations to maintain vigilance and implement proactive strategies, reducing reliance on reactive measures once an outbreak occurs.

The lessons of COVID-19 highlight the importance of continued vigilance, transparency, and collaboration in global health. Although we may never fully understand the origins of COVID-19, the quest for answers has illuminated the critical role of international cooperation in pandemic response. As governments and health organizations reflect on these experiences, they are likely to encounter similar debates, challenges, and obstacles. Yet, there is hope that the enduring legacy of COVID-19 will include stronger health systems, improved data-sharing frameworks, and an unwavering commitment to uncovering the roots of infectious diseases. These steps, while complex, are essential to ensuring that the world is better prepared for the next pandemic—whenever and however it may emerge.

www.ingramcontent.com/pod-product-compliance
Lightning Source LLC
Chambersburg PA
CBHW061423160726
47995CB00003B/734